95

D1261756

1

THE LEGAL PROPERTY RELATIONS OF MARRIED PARTIES

STUDIES IN HISTORY, ECONOMICS AND PUBLIC LAW

EDITED BY THE FACULTY OF POLITICAL SCIENCE OF
COLUMBIA UNIVERSITY

VOLUME XIII]   [NUMBER 1

THE LEGAL PROPERTY RELATIONS
OF MARRIED PARTIES

A STUDY IN COMPARATIVE LEGISLATION

BY

ISIDOR LOEB

AMS PRESS
NEW YORK

COLUMBIA UNIVERSITY
STUDIES IN THE
SOCIAL SCIENCES

34

The Series was formerly known as *Studies in History,
Economics and Public Law.*

Reprinted with the permission of Columbia University Press
From the edition of 1900, New York
First AMS EDITION published 1968
Manufactured in the United States of America

Library of Congress Catalogue Card Number: 68-56668

AMS PRESS, INC.
New York, N.Y. 10003

PREFACE.

THIS comparison of legislation was undertaken during the winter of 1894–95. The pressure of other duties delayed the completion of the work. The examination of the law in most of the states has been brought down to the close of the legislative year 1898; in some instances the legislation of 1899 has been examined.

I desire to express my thanks to many persons from whom I have received assistance and suggestions during the progress of this investigation. I am especially indebted to Professor Munroe Smith, of Columbia University, under whose direction my studies in jurisprudence were prosecuted. It is fitting that I make special mention also of my indebtedness to Professor E. R. A. Seligman, of Columbia University, and to my friend and colleague, Professor Frederick C. Hicks.

ISIDOR LOEB.

BERLIN, *February 25, 1900.*

TABLE OF CONTENTS.

CHAPTER IV.

Systems of Individual Property.

DIVISION I.

Exclusive Rights of the Husband.

DIVISION II.

Marital Administration and Usufruct.

DIVISION III.

System of Dowry.

PART III.

SUCCESSION OF MARRIED PARTIES.

THE LEGAL PROPERTY RELATIONS OF MARRIED PARTIES.

§ 1. *General Introduction.*

The nineteenth century has witnessed great changes in the field of matrimonial property relations. Old systems have been subjected to profound modifications by the introduction of new principles, while, in some instances, local customs and statutes have given place to a common system, thereby reducing the great diversity in the rules of family law. This consolidation of the systems was influenced by the general codification movement in continental Europe, but the change in the case of matrimonial property rights is of especial significance because of the great lack of uniformity that had previously existed in this field of private law.

The changes in the property relations of husband and wife have not, however, been due exclusively to the combination of the systems. The development of new conceptions of the individual and of the family has led to a modification of the old systems and the appearance of new regulations in the field of family relations. With this development there has appeared a tendency to make the new rules general in their character. Universality, however, is not as yet a characteristic of the rules of family law. The interests involved are not as general as those which are affected by the law of obligations and other branches of property law. The peculiar social and religious views and customs of a community determine the family organization and regulate the system of property relations between the married parties. In the earlier stages only family property exists and there are no true matrimonial property relations. With social development disintegration arises within the family. The religious unity is weakened, and, ultimately, with increased industrial development the economic unity is also impaired. Institutions which have been based upon such unity must likewise become modified, a process illustrated by the history of matrimonial property rights in Roman law. Modern codes are passing through a similar development, as is evidenced by the results of the legislative activity of the nineteenth century.

In England and the United States the legal economic relations of married parties have been revolutionized. The fundamental rules of the common law respecting the property and capacity of married women have been abrogated or greatly modified. The changes in the industrial system had affected the economic organization of the family, and it was inevitable that the legal relations should accommodate themselves to the new conditions. At a time when women were acquiring an independent activity it was natural that particular attention should be called to the inequalities to which the law subjected them. Among the arguments advanced against the old system was the charge that that it was based upon the principle of natural inequality of the sexes and of masculine superiority. The reformers demanded not only the restriction of the husband's extensive rights in his wife's property, but also the removal of the disabilities which were imposed upon married women. In general, no account was taken of the fact that some of these disabilities had their historical justification in the desire to preserve the unity of the family, and had not necessarily been influenced by considerations of the natural incapacity of the woman. Moreover, the fact that the same motive had led to the imposition of duties and disabilities upon the husband was frequently disregarded. The personality of the woman and not the relation into which she had entered was considered the true source of her disabilities.

In the early acts no attempt was made at a general revision and codification of the law governing the economic relations of married parties. The legislatures were without models by which to form the new measures, and the full effects of the modifications were not appreciated. The married women's acts confined themselves to the removal of the disabilities of the wife. They did not, in general, deprive her of the exemptions and privileges which she had enjoyed on account of these disabilities, nor was the husband relieved of his previous duties and burdens. As a result, the matrimonial property systems became characterized by gross inequalities and inconsistencies. The husband, though he received no property from the wife, might be held liable for her ante-nuptial debts. His creditors could not obtain satisfaction out of the wife's property, even though, as a matter of fact, the debts had been contracted for the support of the wife. Under the new conditions it was possible for a woman possessing considerable property in her own right to obtain a divorce on the ground of lack of support. A married woman who had been accorded full capacity for carrying on legal proceedings might still be able to plead the fact of coverture as a bar to the running of the period of the limitation of actions. Moreover, while the husband had been deprived of rights in the property of his wife, the latter retained the privileges which she had possessed in his real property.

In undertaking to grant equal rights to the wife the legislature had produced a new inequality, which threatened to destroy the ethical unity of the family. The Roman law, under the influence of similar conditions of economic and social development, came to recognize the equality of married parties in respect to property rights. The regulation of the relations of the parties, however, was determined more logically in accordance with such principle of equality. The later legislation in the United States has removed many of the inconsistencies of the earlier statutes. In general, there is exhibited a marked tendency to carry out the strict principle of equality in defining the legal economic relations of the married parties.

The legislations of continental Europe have felt the influence of the new ideas and conditions. The modifications of matrimonial property law have not, however, been as radical as in the case of England and the United States. The explanation is to be found in the fact that the property rights of the wife in continental countries were, in general, superior to those recognized by the English common law. Some modifications have been made in connection with the adoption of the modern codes which have taken the place of the particular laws of local communities. This is particularly true of the civil code of the German Empire, which received legislative approval in 1896 and went into effect on January 1, 1900. A draft code which has been prepared for Switzerland will, if enacted, produce similar results. In some of the older codes important modifications of matrimonial property rights have been made by subsequent statutes, and movements directed to like ends are in active operation in a number of states.

The writer proposes to consider the general principles of the matrimonial property systems which obtain at present in the United States and in the chief states of Europe. Particular attention will be given to recent legislative changes. All of the systems have certain common aims, and there appears an increasing tendency towards the development of common regulations for the realization of these ends. The extent to which this tendency has been realized will appear in this comparison of existing legislation.

The consideration of this subject falls under three divisions. In the first will be presented the general effects of marriage upon the capacities and relations of the parties, independent of the particular system of property rights which may obtain.   In the second, the chief forms which have been developed for the regulation of matrimonial property relations will be considered.   And, finally, the relations of succession between married parties, as essential to an adequate appreciation of matrimonial property rights, will be discussed.

PART I.

EFFECTS OF MARRIAGE UPON LEGAL CAPACITY.

§ 2. *General Legal Capacity of Acting.*

THE personal status of married parties in their relation to each other and to third parties is closely connected with the system of matrimonial property rights. Thus, the capacity for performing legal acts is affected by the character of the property relations existing between the married parties. For example, where the law accords the husband extensive privileges in his wife's property, provisions will generally be found by which the married woman's capacity of acting is so restricted as to preserve the rights of the husband. In like manner, the rules governing the property relations of husband and wife may be influenced by the prevailing conception of personal capacity of the parties.

The marriage is not regarded as imposing any general incapacity of acting upon the man. On the other hand, all legislations have, at some time, recognized the general legal incapacity of the married woman. The early Roman and Teutonic laws take this position and consider the incapacity as flowing from the husband's power over the wife. Force is a cardinal element in all primitive legislation, and affects family as well as economic relations. This is illustrated by the fact that the marriage is regarded as resting upon a forcible seizure or sale.[1]

The incapacity of the married woman was similar to that which affected her as a child. At Roman law she passed from the *patria potestas* to the *manus mariti*. Under Teutonic law the *Mund* of her father or guardian was exchanged for that of her husband. The former emphasized the power and right of the man, the latter placed stress upon the element of guardianship. In both systems, however, the complete unity of the family, under the authority of its head, excluded any general independent activity of the other members.

The Roman law developed an informal free marriage without *manus* and, by the last century of the Republic, this had become the normal system. As a result of the absence of *manus mariti*, the legal personality of the wife was no longer merged in that of the husband. Personal relations arose between the husband and wife. The marriage, as such, was not regarded as affecting the woman's general capacity of performing legal acts.[2] This is the position of the modern Roman law.[3]

Primitive Teutonic law developed into a number of different systems. As a rule, however, the general incapacity of the married woman was continued. The reception of the Roman law was limited in the field of family relations and the principle of the general legal capacity of the wife found but slight application. The guardianship of unmarried women gradually disappeared. In the case of the married woman, however, the husband appeared as a sort of permanent natural guardian and the existing matrimonial property relations strengthened this conception.

---

[1] Sohm, *Inst.*, § 92; Schröder, *Lehrbuch*, p. 67 *seq.;* Heusler, *Inst.*, vol. ii, § 130.

[2] Sohm, *Inst.*, § 93.   [3] Windscheid, *Pandekten*, vol. ii, §§ 490, 491.

In the present century there has been a tendency to regard the general capacity of the woman as remaining unaffected by the marriage. This principle, which is at the basis of the Austrian and Russian codes, has been accepted by the new code of Germany[4] and by the Norwegian statute of 1888 which regulates the property relations between married parties.[5] The other continental countries have, in general, preserved the principle that the wife, as such, is under a general disability in respect to her legal capacity of acting. It must not be assumed, however, that the married woman's activity is entirely unrestricted in the one case or that it is completely subject to control in the other. The two classes are distinguished by the fact that in the former the wife has perfect freedom of activity in so far as she is not limited by positive provisions, while in the latter class she has legal capacity of acting only to the extent that this is specifically accorded to her.

England and many of the American states have practically taken the former position. In so far, however, as the common law disabilities of coverture have not been expressly abrogated, it is the rule of interpretation to regard the married woman as restricted in her legal activity to the extent that the law has not accorded her positive privileges. Accordingly, most of the legislations contain specific grants of power to the married woman.[6]

The disabilities to which married women are subjected are explained on various grounds. Some consider the control as the survival of the guardianship of the family or the clan. According to this view it is exercised on account of the weakness and inexperience of the sex. Others reject the assump-

---

[4] *Motive*, vol. iv, pp. 112, 113; *Denkschrift*, p. 268.

[5] Stat. June 29, 1888, arts. 11, 19, *An. étran.*, vol, 18, p. 766.

[6] For examples of total abrogation of common law, see in Appendix, note A, *Miss. Const.*, § 94, *An. Code*, §2289.

tion of natural incapacity and regard the legal disabilities of the wife as justified by considerations of the unity of the family. The legislations have not logically followed either of the above conceptions. It is true that in some states some one principle may have exercised a predominant influence. At the same time disabilities exist which can be explained only by reference to other considerations. Thus the prevailing system of matrimonial property relations, including the liability of the husband for the obligations of the wife, has generally exercised considerable influence upon the conception of the legal capacity of the married woman. Recent legislation, however, clearly indicates a tendency to impose restrictions upon the legal activity of married parties only so far as these may be necessary to promote the ethical unity of the marriage. Specific limitations will then arise according to the particular system which the parties select for the determination of their property relations.

§ 3. *General Contractual Capacity of the Married Woman.*

The absence of any single, uniform principle as the basis of the legal incapacity of the married woman is clearly indicated by the provisions of the French Civil Code which limit the wife's general contractual capacity. The married woman cannot give, alienate, pledge or acquire unless the husband joins in the act or accords his written authorization of the same.[1] Upon the refusal of the husband to grant the necessary consent, the wife may be authorized by the court to perform the act.[2] These provisions may be justified from considerations of conjugal unity, though the power of the wife to appeal from the decision of the head of the family is a departure from the strict principle.

It is provided, however, that the husband cannot grant the wife any general authority to act in these matters. A

---

[1] C. C., 217.   [2] *Ibid.*, 219.

special authorization is essential for each act.[3]   Moreover, if the husband is incapacitated by reason of disappearance, minority, interdiction or criminal punishment, the wife requires a judicial authorization before she can enter into contracts.[4]   These requirements cannot be explained upon the principle of unity of family administration.   Under such a principle, where the husband is disqualified the wife must appear as the proper administrator if she is recognized as possessing the natural capacity to fulfill these functions. Upon the same assumption the husband would not be prevented from granting the wife a general power of acting with respect to certain matters.   Having satisfied himself respecting the wife's ability, he would delegate the administration to her in the same manner as a party might authorize an agent to represent him generally in certain relations.

On the other hand, the inexperience and natural incapacity of the woman cannot be accepted as the uniform principle, since the code does not impose any general restrictions upon dispositions between the husband and wife.   Marriage agreements cannot be contracted or altered after the celebration of the marriage, but it does not appear that this restriction limits ordinary dispositions between the parties, and, in any event, the wife, with the marital authorization, may make contracts with third parties, from which benefits will accrue to the husband.

The combination of different principles is manifested finally in the recognition of acts of the wife, performed without the marital authorization, as *negotia claudicantia* and hence voidable and not void.   Third parties cannot take advantage of the defect of authority, but such plea may be advanced not only by the husband and his heirs, but also by the wife and her representatives.[5]

---

[3] C. C., 223.   [4] *Ibid.*, 221, 222, 224.   [5] *Ibid.*, 225.

It is worthy of note that the French legislature has in recent years enacted statutes similar in nature to those which marked the beginning of the contractual capacity of married women in English and American law.[6]   Thus, a married woman has been given the right to make deposits in savings banks, etc., though she cannot withdraw the same if the husband objects to such disposition.[7]   An act of 1899 provides that a married woman may become a member of mutual benefit associations, but she must obtain the marital authorization before she can participate in the administration of such societies.[8]

Reference to the prevailing matrimonial property system is essential to a due appreciation of the regulations concerning marital authorization.   The system of community of property which obtains in France has had great influence in determining the general contractual capacity of the married woman.   Where the wife has separate property a more or less extensive power of contracting with reference to the same is accorded her by the French, as well as other systems that require the marital authorization.[9]

The European legislations which have been most directly influenced by the French code have, in general, retained the principle of marital authorization, but have defined it more consistently and have introduced modifications in the direction of a greater freedom of activity for the wife.   This is particularly true of the Italian and Spanish codes.   The draft code of Italy, submitted in 1862, proposed to accord general legal capacity to the married woman.[10]   While this principle was not accepted, the marital authorization was con-

---

[6] *Cf. post*, § 37.

[7] Stat., Apl. 9, 1881, art. 6, *Bull. des lois*, xii Sér., vol. 22, p. 666; Stat. July 20, 1886, art. 13, *ibid.*, vol. 33, p. 279.

[8] Stat., Apl. 1, 1899, art. 3, Sirey, *Recueil*, 1899, p. 729.

[9] See *post*, § 42.   [10] Huc, *Code Civil Italien*, p. 66.

siderably limited.   Thus, the husband may grant the wife a
general authorization to enter into contracts.[11]   Moreover, if
the husband is incapacitated by reason of minority, judicially
declared disappearance, *etc.*, the marital authorization is not
required.[12]   As in the French code, the court may always
supply the consent of the husband.[13]

The Italian code protects the wife against the undue influence of her husband by requiring the authorization of the court
for acts of the wife in cases where her interests are opposed to
those of her husband.[14]   The Spanish code, on the contrary,
does not regard the married woman as subject to undue influence or any natural incapacity.   No particular provisions
are made for her protection in ordinary contracts with her
husband.   Moreover, the wife cannot plead incapacity or
defect of authority, such privilege being accorded only to
the husband and his heirs, and existing solely in the interests
of the marital administration.[15]

The code of Louisiana[16] has followed the provisions of the
French legislation, but has given a clearer recognition to the
natural incapacity of the woman by the requirement for judicial authorization of acts by which the wife undertakes to
bind her individual property.[17]   It is considered necessary
to protect the wife against the husband as well as against
third parties.   On the other hand, the influence of the legislation in other American states is to be seen in recent statutes according the married woman the right to subscribe for
stock in building and loan associations, to make deposits in

---

[11] Italy, C. C., 134; the Spanish code does not prohibit such grants of authority

[12] Italy, C. C., 135; Spain, C. C., 188. *Cf. ibid.*, 1441.

[13] Italy, C. C., 136; Spain, C. C., 60, 61.

[14] C. C., 136.   [15] C. C., 65.

[16] C. C., 122, 125, 132–134.

[17] C. C., 126–128. *Cf. ibid.*, 129.

banks and to withdraw and to transfer the same, without the intervention of her husband, as if she were a *femme sole*.[18]

The Swiss cantons, in general, limit the contractual capacity of married women. Some of the cantons still retain the guardianship of women, and others, in providing for the emancipation of women in general, except the married woman from the benefit of such acts. The interests of the family administration have been the chief cause for the continuation of such disability. Separate property of the married woman is recognized in a number of the cantons, and, where this exists the wife is accorded a certain power of contracting in reference to such property.[19] Most of the legislations, however, do not relieve the wife from her disabilities in case the husband is incapacitated from acting. She continues under guardianship, her acts requiring the consent of the husband's curator or of some other authorized party. In the majority of the cantons it is likewise considered necessary to protect the wife against the undue influence of the husband. Accordingly it is required that she shall be assisted by a guardian *ad hoc* in order to conclude certain kinds of contracts, particularly those in which the husband has an interest in the matter concerning which the agreement is made.[20]

The draft Swiss code represents an attempt to harmonize and combine the conflicting rules. The modern principle is followed in that the contractual capacity of the married wo-

[18] Acts, 1894, no. 74; *ibid.*, 1896, no. 63.

[19] Basle, Stat. Mch. 10, 1884, art. 30 *seq.*, *An. étran.*, vol. 14, p. 552; Glaris, L. B., ii, 174, 175, *ibid.*, vol. 4, p. 518; Lucerne, Stat. Nov. 26, 1880, arts. 11, 16, 22, *ibid.*, vol. 10, pp. 487, 488; Zürich, P. R. G., § 597; Lardy, *Législations Suisses*, pp. 65, 125, 160, 239, 263. *Cf. post*, § 42.

[20] Lucerne, Stat. Nov. 26, 1880, art. 16; Zürich, P. R. G., §§ 599, 600; Lardy, *Législations Suisses*, pp. 28, 67, 125, 126, 190, 225, 278, 303, 333, 348; *contra*, Basle, Stat. Oct. 16, 1876, art. 5, *An. étran.*, vol. 6, p. 571, where the old rule is partially abrogated.

man is made to depend upon the particular system of matrimonial property relations which obtains between the parties. Following the majority of the cantonal legislations, however, the draft code starts with the principle of general incapacity. The wife, aside from her functions of household administratration,[21] has contractual capacity only to the extent that this is recognized by the system which governs the economic relations of the married parties.[22] An exception arises with respect to the separate property of the wife. Under all of the systems she possesses the power of contracting generally with reference to such property.[23] Under the draft code the wife possesses the right of exercising an industry or occupation, but the husband in the interest of the conjugal unity is given the right of forbidding the same. The prohibition of the husband may be rescinded by the court if the wife shows that just cause does not exist for such action.[24] The possibility of undue influence by the husband is also recognized, and hence the authorization of the court is required for certain acts of the wife.[25]

The Prussian and Saxon codes[26] require the marital authorization for the contracts of the wife which may affect the unity of the family or the matrimonial property.[27] Such authorization, however, is not necessary for ordinary contracts respecting the separate property of married women.[28] Moreover, the wife is recognized as having the first right to the matrimonial administration in case the husband is inca-

[21] *Post,* § 8.

[22] Switz, *Vorentwurf,* 212.   [23] *Ibid.,* 215, 269.   [24] *Ibid.,* 186.   [25] *Ibid.,* 214.

[26] These codes, as well as the other legislations obtaining among the members of the German federal union, were displaced by the national code on Jan. 1, 1900. For the purposes of the present comparison they will be treated as existing legislations.

[27] Prussia, A. L. R., ii, 1, §§ 196, 320, 377; Saxony, B. G., §1638.

[28] Prussia, A. L. R., ii, 1, §§ 221, 222, 318; Saxony, B. G., §§ 1640, 1693.

pacitated from acting.[29]   The Prussian legislation, however, places particular limitations upon contracts between married parties.   These must be executed before a judge whose duty it is to see that advantage is not taken of the wife.   If this requirement is not observed, the wife may acquire rights but will not become subject to any obligation as a result of the agreement with the husband.[30]

The new code of Germany starts with the principle that the contractual capacity of a woman is not affected by her marriage.[31]   This general principle is modified in the interests of the conjugal unity by the provision that the husband, unless he has consented to the same, may secure the rescission, for the future, of such agreements as require personal service on the part of the wife.[32]   Before the act will be abrogated the authorization of the court must be obtained.   Such authorization must be accorded if the act injuriously affects the marital interests.   The same authority may supply the consent of the husband if the latter, by reason of illness or absence, is unable to assent to the act or if his refusal appears unwarranted.   The fact that this control over the contracts of the married woman is based upon the desire to preserve the conjugal unity is further indicated by the provision that it may be exercised by a husband who has not attained his majority, but cannot be employed by the latter's guardian or representative.[33]

An interesting development may be noted by comparing the provisions of the three preliminary drafts of the code with those indicated above.   The first draft made all contracts whereby the wife obligated herself for personal service

[29] Prussia, A. L. R., ii, 1, §§ 202–204, 261, 325–327; Saxony, B. G., §§ 1684, 1700.

[30] A. L. R., ii, 1, §§ 198–201.

[31] See *ante*, § 2, note 4.

[32] Germany, B. G., § 1358.   [33] *Ibid.*

absolutely dependent upon the consent of the husband, but provided that the husband alone could attack the validity of agreements that lacked the proper authorization.[34] The second and third drafts recognized the principle, established in the code as adopted, that such acts of the wife are valid without marital authorization, and that the court could supply the husband's consent under the circumstances above noted. But the husband was given the unrestricted right of abrogating such acts for the future, even if he had consented to the same or if his consent had been supplied by the proper authority.[35] Starting with such acts of the wife dependent upon the will of the husband, the close of the development finds the married woman free to enter into such contracts. The husband, with the previous authorization of the court, is enabled to revoke the agreements for the future, provided his consent to the same has not been accorded directly or through the agency of the judge.

Aside from this limitation, the general contractual capacity of the married woman is limited only as regards her power of affecting the matrimonial property.[36] Acts of the wife affecting her separate property are subject to no particular limitations, and the same is true of contracts between the husband and wife.[37]

The compilers of the German code were influenced by the Roman conception of the wife's contractual capacity. The Roman law contains no particular provisions respecting the

---

[34] I. *Entwurf,* § 1277.

[35] II. *Entwurf,* § 1258; III. *Entwurf,* § 1341.

[36] See *post,* §§ 20, 21, 27, 42.

[37] In case of the bankruptcy of a married party, the contracts made with his spouse in the preceding year, whether before or after the marriage, are attackable by the creditors so far as they are damaged thereby and the other party does not prove that he did not know of the intention of the common debtor to damage his creditor's interests. Germany, *Konkursordnung,* § 31, R. G. Bl., 1898, pp. 618, 619.

ordinary contracts of married women. It was not found
necessary to limit her capacity of affecting the matrimonial
property. The husband's rights in the dowry were originally those of an owner, and even after the legislation of the
Empire he continued to be regarded as the formal owner
during the marriage.[38]   The Roman law likewise imposed
no limitations upon ordinary contracts between the husband
and wife.[39]

The Austrian[40] and Russian[41] codes accept the general
principles of the Roman law respecting the contracts of
married women, and in Norway, practically the same condition obtains, the power of the wife to conclude ordinary
contracts being unrestricted except with reference to her
capacity of binding the matrimonial property.[42]

Under the English common law system marriage destroys
the general contractual capacity of the woman. She cannot
contract even with the consent or joinder of her husband.
Different explanations of the origin and basis of this rule
have been advanced. The conception that marriage unites
the man and woman in one person has exercised a great
influence upon the development of the law governing the
relations of husband and wife.[43]   This legal fiction, however,
will not serve to explain the disabilities of married women.
Recent investigations tend to prove that the early law did
not regard the contractual capacity of the woman as destroyed by the marriage, but that such incapacity developed
as a result of the fact that she ceased to possess property

---

[38] See *post*, § 32.

[39] Sohm, *Inst.*, § 94; Windscheid, *Pandekten*, vol. ii, § 491.

[40] Certain contracts between husband and wife must be concluded before a
notary. Stat. July 25, 1871, R. G. Bl., no. 76.

[41] Leuthold, *R. R.*, pp. 59, 60.

[42] See *post*, §§ 20, 21.

[43] Black, *Comm.*, vol. i, p. 442; Kent, *Comm.*, vol. ii, p. 129.

which could be bound by her contracts.[44] The general
principle governing the incapacity of the married woman
appears to be the desire to preserve the unity of the family
and the administration of the matrimonial property. Hence,
if the husband is banished or is regarded as dead in the eyes
of the law, as in the case of imprisonment for life, the wife
possesses general contractual capacity.[45] There are, however, exceptions to the general principle. For example,
abandonment of the wife by the husband, which is not accompanied by his departure from and loss of residence in
the state, does not have the effect of removing her disabilities.[46] This constituted one of the greatest hardships of the
common law, and was largely instrumental in bringing
about the statutory modifications. The fact that the married
woman cannot contract with her husband nor enter into
engagements with third parties, even if the marital authorization has been obtained, represents another departure from
the general principle. Such limitations cannot be explained
from considerations of family unity. On the contrary, they
develop serious obstacles to the efficient administration of the
matrimonial property, and cumbrous processes were invented
in order to evade their provisions.

The rules established under the equitable jurisdiction of the
courts are, however, based upon the general principle indicated above. Contracts, affecting the wife personally, which
might impair the conjugal unity, are not valid in equity any
more than at common law. But the English chancery courts
recognized the power of the married woman to possess a
separate estate, free from the common law rights of the

---

[44] Pol. and Mait., *Hist.*, vol. ii, p. 432; Florence G. Buckstaff, "Married
Women's Property in Anglo-Saxon Law" *An. Amer. Acad.*, vol. iv, p. 247 *seq.*;
Ernest Young, "The Anglo-Saxon Family Law," *Essays in Anglo-Saxon Law*,
p. 176 *seq.*

[45] Kent, *Comm.*, vol. ii, p. 155 *seq.*   [46] *Ibid.*

husband. With respect to such property the wife could contract as if she were a *femme sole*, subject to such limitations upon her capacity as were contained in the act of settlement.[47] The fear of undue influence on the part of the husband led to the recognition of certain limitations which would not bind the unmarried woman. The most famous of these limitations is the restraint upon anticipation, intended to prevent the woman, under marital influence, from destroying or disposing of the capital of her separate estate.[48]

The effect of the married women's property acts has been to extend the general contractual capacity of the wife. In England, as early as 1856, an attempt was made to accord to the married woman a general power of making contracts, but it was not until 1868 that a bill passed the House of Commons granting her the general right to contract as if unmarried, subject to limitations with respect to particular matters.[49] The bill encountered severe opposition in the House of Lords, as a result of which important modifications were made. As finally enacted the wife was not accorded general contractual capacity. The married woman was given a limited statutory separate estate with power of disposition over the same.[50] The Married Woman's Property Act of 1882 extended the scope of the separate estate of the wife and accorded her a general power of contracting in respect of and to the extent of the same, as if she were a *femme sole*.[51] It was provided that every contract of a married woman should be deemed to have been entered into with reference to her separate property unless the contrary be shown.[52] Finally, an act of

[47] *Ibid.*, p. 163 *seq*. This is the view generally accepted in England and the United States. An opposing view is that she has only such capacity as is granted under the terms upon which the estate was settled.

[48] Schouler, *H. & W.*, § 202; *cf. post*, note 53.

[49] *Bull. Lég. comp.*, 1871, p. 15.   [50] Act 33 & 34 Vict., c. 93.

[51] Act 45 & 46 Vict., c. 75, § 1 (1), (2).   [52] *Ibid.*, § 1 (3).

1893 completed the development by repealing the above clause and raising an absolute presumption that the contracts of the married woman are made in respect to her separate property, whether she is or is not entitled to any such estate at the time when she enters into the agreement.[53] Such contracts, moreover, bind all of her property after discoverture.[54]

In the United States the movement to give validity to the contracts of married women commenced at an earlier date than in England. In the first part of the nineteenth century acts were passed conferring contractual capacity upon married women who were abandoned by their husbands. Later, married women in general were granted power to contract in relation to certain property to which was given the character of a statutory separate estate.[55] These specific grants have been gradually enlarged, until the close of the century finds many of the states recognizing that married women have general contractual capacity, while those that still maintain the general common law rule have nullified it, to a great extent, by numerous exceptions. The legislation has been so extensive and, at times, so inconsistent and contradictory, that it becomes a difficult matter to indicate the exact position of each state. A general classification will be sufficient to indicate the prevailing tendency. The individual legislations will fall into one of two divisions according as they have or have not accorded general contractual capacity to the married woman. In the first class, limitations may be placed upon certain kinds of contracts, while in the second class more or less extensive specific grants

---

[53] Act 56 & 57 Vict., c. 63, §§ 1 (a), 4. It was expressly provided, however, that no such contract should be binding upon separate property which the wife is restrained from anticipating, though such property may be bound by the costs of judicial proceedings which she institutes (*ibid.*, §§ 1 (c), 2).

[54] *Ibid.*, § 1 (c).   [55] See *post*, § 37.

of capacity are made. In the following states and territories the married woman is recognized as possessing
general contractual capacity:[56] Alabama,[57] Arizona,[58] Cali-
ornia,[59] Colorado,[60] Connecticut,[61] Delaware,[62] Idaho,[63] Illinois,[64] Indiana,[65] Iowa,[66] Kansas,[67] Kentucky,[68] Maine,[69]
Maryland,[70] Massachusetts,[71] Minnesota,[72] Mississippi,[73] Missouri,[74] Montana,[75] Nebraska,[76] Nevada,[77] New Hampshire,[78]

[56] For limitations upon capacity to make particular contracts, see *post*, §§ 4, 5,
20, 21, 42.

[57] Code, 1896, § 2526. The Code of 1886 limited this capacity to contracts in
writing entered into with the written consent of the husband.

[58] R. S., 1887, §§ 2103, 2104.

[59] Subject in contracts with husband to general rules respecting contracts between persons occupying confidential relations. C. C., 158. *Cf.* Stat. & Amend.,
1891, p. 137; *ibid.*, 1895, p. 53.

[60] An. St., 1891, § 3021.

[61] So far as regards third persons. G. S., 1888, § 2796.

[62] Laws, vol. 14, c. 550, §§ 2–4, in R. C., 1893, p. 600.

[63] R. S., 1887, §§ 2504, 2508.

[64] An. St., 1885, c. 68, ¶ 6. But transfers between husband and wife to be
valid as against third persons must be publicly recorded (*ibid.*, ¶ 9).

[65] An. St., 1894, § 6960.

[66] Code, 1897, § 3164.

[67] G. S., 1889, § 3759.

[68] Stat., 1894, § 2128. Same qualification as in Illinois. See *ante*, note 64.

[69] R. S., 1883, c. 61, §§ 1, 2, 4.

[70] Laws, 1898, c. 457, §§ 4, 5.

[71] But she is not authorized to contract with husband. P. S., 1882, c. 147, § 2.

[72] G. S., 1894, §§ 5530, 5532.

[73] An. Code, 1892, § 2289. Limitations exist upon certain contracts between
husband and wife. *Ibid.*, §§ 2293, 2294.

[74] R. S., 1899, § 4335.

[75] C. C., 1895, §§ 214, 256. Same qualification as in Cal. See *ante*, note 59.

[76] To same extent as a married man. C. S., 1891, § 1412.

[77] G. S., 1885, § 517. Same qualification as in Cal. See *ante*, note 59.

[78] P. S., 1891, c. 176, § 2.

New Jersey,[79] New York,[80] North Dakota,[81] Ohio,[82] Oklahoma,[83] Oregon,[84] Pennsylvania,[85] Rhode Island,[86] South Carolina,[87] South Dakota,[88] Utah,[89] Vermont,[90] Washington,[91] Wyoming[92] and Hawaii.[93]

The following legislations have not entirely abrogated the general incapacity of the married woman to enter into con-

[79] Act Mch. 27, 1874, § 5, Rev., 1877, p. 637; but not authorized thereby to contract with husband (*ibid.*, § 14), though she may assign policies of life insurance to him (*ibid.*, § 19).

[80] Laws, 1896, c. 272, § 21.

[81] R. C., 1895, § 2767.

[82] R. S., 1891, §§ 3112, 4107. Same qualification as in Cal. See *ante*, note 59.

[83] R. S., 1893, § 2968. Same qualification as in Cal. See *ante*, note 59.

[84] An. St., 1887, § 2997.

[85] Laws, 1893, p. 344, §§ 1, 2.

[86] An act of 1893 provided that a married woman could make any contract the same as if she were single (Acts, 1892–93, c. 1204). The Revision of 1896 returned to the common law rule of incapacity with numerous positive grants of capacity (G. L., 1896, c. 194, §§ 3, 4). In the same year an act of the legislature repealed the positive grants of power to contract and restored the general principle of act of 1893 (Acts, 1896–97, c. 335).

[87] The new constitution of 1895, art. xvii, § 9, introduces this rule. Before its enactment the married woman could make contracts with reference to her separate estate as if unmarried. C. S. L., 1893, § 2167.

[88] C. L., 1887, § 2590. Same qualification as in Cal. See *ante*, note 59.

[89] R. S., 1898, §§ 1199, 1200.

[90] Except in agreements with her husband. Stat., 1894, § 2644.

[91] G. S., 1891, § 1409.

[92] Laws, 1888, c. 59, § 1. Before this act her capacity was limited to contracts entered into with reference to her property. R. S., 1887, § 1559.

[93] Except that contracts for personal services require the written consent of her husband and she is not authorized to contract with her husband. Laws, 1888, c. xi, § 2.

tracts : Arkansas,[94] Florida,[95] Georgia,[96] Michigan,[97] New
Mexico,[98] North Carolina,[99] Tennessee,[100] Texas,[101] Virginia,[102]

[91] She may make contracts respecting her separate estate and services, and may
effect insurance policies upon the life of her husband.   Dig. Stat., 1894, §§ 4944–
4946.

[95] She may charge her estate in equity for purchase price and for agreements
made for its benefit (Const., art. xi, § 2); dispose of her earnings (R. S., 1892,
§ 2075); control her deposits in banks (*ibid.*, § 2119); and subscribe for stock
in building and loan associations (*ibid.*, § 2208).

[96] She may contract with reference to her separate estate (Code, 1895, § 2488),
but the consent of the court is essential to the validity of contracts that she may
make with her husband or trustee (*ibid.*, § 2490).

[97] She may contract respecting her separate property.   An. St., 1882, § 6295.

[98] With consent of husband she may make any contract which she might make
if unmarried (C. L., 1897, § 1510).   She may contract with her husband as if unmarried (*ibid.*, § 1511).

[99] Husband's written authorization is essential to validity of all contracts affecting her property except those made for personal expenses, support of family or to
pay ante-nuptial debts (Code, 1883, § 1826).   Contracts between husband and
wife which affect latter's property for a longer period than three years, require
special form (*ibid.*, § 1835), but other contracts between them, not contrary to
good morals, are valid (*ibid.*, § 1836).

[100] No statutory separate estate exists.   The married woman may freely dispose
of such property as is settled upon her for her separate use (Code, 1884, § 3350).
She may contract in writing so as to bind her property with mechanics' lien
(*ibid.*, § 2741); may effect insurance on husband's life (*ibid.*, § 3336); may make
deposits in banks (*ibid.*, § 1729); and may hold stock in building and loan associations (*ibid.*, § 1757).

[101] She may contract for necessaries for herself and children and for expenses
for benefit of her separate property (R. S., 1895, art. 2970).   She may contract
so as to bind benevolent associations of which she is a member (*ibid.*, art. 644),
and where appointed executrix, *etc.*, may give bond which shall bind her separate
property (*ibid.*, arts. 1947, 2604).

[102] She may make contracts with respect to her labor or separate estate as if she
were a *femme sole*.   Code, 1887, §§ 2286, 2288.

West Virginia,[103] Wisconsin [104] and the District of Columbia.[105]

§ 4. *Power of the Married Woman to become Surety for another Person.*

Some states, while according the married woman a general capacity of contracting, limit her power to enter into specific kinds of agreements. This is particularly true of contracts whereby she undertakes to answer for the debt or liability of another person. Many of those legislations, also, which make the marital authorization requisite to the validity of the wife's contracts, place additional restrictions upon her contracts of surety.

Here, feminine weakness is the determining factor. The inexperience of the woman and the probability that her confidence, which she so freely accords, may be taken advantage of, are the chief considerations at the basis of such provisions. Thus, the famous *senatus consultum Velleianum*, passed in the reign of Claudius, applied to unmarried as well as married women.[1] The *intercessio* of a woman was prohibited. It was necessary, however, for the woman to appeal to the praetor for an *exceptio* where it was sought to enforce such acts against her.[2]   This equitable relief was

[103] She may dispose of her separate estate as if single (Acts, 1893, c. iii, §§ 2, 3); may make deposits in banks and withdraw same (*ibid.*, § 8); may become stockholder in any company, except mutual life insurance companies (*ibid.*, § 9); and may insure husband's life for her own benefit (*ibid.*, § 5).

[104] She may dispose of her separate estate as if single (An. St., 1889, § 2342; Laws, 1895, c. 86); may make deposits in banks and withdraw same (An. St., 1889, § 2020; *cf.* Laws, 1895, c. 160, § 1) and may contract policies of life insurance (Laws, 1891, c. 376).

[105] She may contract in reference to her property in the same manner as if unmarried (Act, June 1, 1896, § 4, U. S. Stat. at Large, vol. 29, p. 193), and may perform any labor or services for her sole and separate account (*ibid.*, § 3).

[1] Dig., 16, 1; Cod., 4, 29.   [2] Sohm, *Inst.*, § 53, p. 269.

not accorded in cases where the conduct of the woman had been such as to prejudice the rights of innocent parties. In this way, as well as through legislation, exceptions to the rule were established.[3]   In the legislation of Justinian a distinction is made between the intercession of a woman for her husband and her intercession for third parties. Thus, a woman's contract of surety may be valid if it has been made in a formal manner, but if it has been entered into by a married woman for the benefit of her husband, it is invalid, notwithstanding the observance of such form, unless it is clearly shown that the money has been applied to the benefit of the wife.[4]

In those legislations which subject the contracts of the wife to marital authorization, no particular provisions are necessary respecting her intercession in behalf of third parties. She is, in general, prevented from engaging herself without the consent of her husband   But, aside from specific limitations, there is no security against the undertaking of such liability for the benefit of her husband, and, in states recognizing the general contractual capacity of the wife, the same is true of her engagements for third parties as well of those which she undertakes for her husband.

Some of the states contain positive prohibitions upon the intercession of married women. The restriction in some legislations applies only to her undertakings for the benefit of her husband,[5] while in others it extends to the assumption of liability for any person.[6]   A number of states recognize

---

[3] Windscheid, *Pandekten*, vol. ii, §§ 485–487. *Cf.* Dig., 16, 1; Cod., 4, 29.

[4] Nov., 134, c. 8; Windscheid, *Pandekten*, vol. ii, §§ 488, 489.

[5] Ala. Code, 1896, § 2529; La., C. C., 126–128, 1790, 2398; N. H., P. S., 1891, c. 176, § 2; Vt., but a mortgage given for such purpose is valid, Stat., 1894, § 2646.

[6] Geo., Code, 1885, § 2488; Ind., An. St., 1894, § 6964; Ky., unless estate is set aside for that purpose by deed or mortgage, Stat., 1894, § 2127; N. J., Act Mch. 27, 1874, § 5, Rev., 1877, p. 637, but if married woman obtains anything of value

the probability of undue influence, but consider that sufficient protection will be accorded the wife if she is given a special guardian in such cases,[7] or if these acts are required to be executed before the court or are made dependent upon judicial authorization.[8] The majority of the legislations, however, contain no particular limitations upon the capacity of the married woman to contract such obligations.[9] The principle followed is that in the normal marriage mutual love and confidence will be sufficient protection for the wife, and that where this condition does not exist, a legal limitation will not furnish adequate security. Under such circumstances means will be found for disposing of the wife's property or obliging her in a different manner for the husband's benefit.

§ 5. *Donations between Married Parties.*

Donations between married parties have been the subject of particular restrictions in most legal systems. Such limitations may be imposed in the interests of third parties, or may be intended to regulate gifts as between the parties themselves. It is a principle, universally recognized, that

on the faith of the contract she will be liable thereon, Act, June 13, 1895, Laws, p. 821; S. C., C. S. L., § 2167; Argovie, Stat. Apl. 29, 1877, art. 1, *An. étran.*, vol. 7, p. 619; Lucerne, Stat. Nov. 26, 1880, art. 16.

[7] *Cf.* references to Swiss cantons, *ante*, § 3, note 20.

[8] Geneva, Lardy, *Législations Suisses*, p. 105; Norway, Stat. June 29, 1888, art. 13; Saxony, B. G., § 1650 *seq. Cf.* Italy, C. C., 136.

[9] *Cf. ante*, § 3. The Prussian *Landrecht* originally contained the requirement for judicial execution of contracts whereby a wife engages herself for the benefit of her husband. This provision was abrogated by a statute of Dec. 1, 1889, which repealed as well the provisions of the common law and provincial statutes concerning the intercession of women. G. S. S., p. 1169. In the Canton of Basle City, a statute of Oct. 16, 1876 (art. 5, *An. étran.*, vol. 6, p. 571), abolished the rule which required that the wife should be assisted by a third party where she becomes surety for her husband. In Russia, a wife cannot draw or assign bills of exchange without husband's consent. Leuthold, *R. R.*, § 24.

transactions made for the purpose of defrauding creditors or purchasers are attackable by such parties. Many systems, however, go further and impute fraud where a debtor makes gratuitous transfers of his property to his spouse or to other members of his family. This principle was introduced in English law by the statute of 13 Elizabeth, c. 5, which has been generally followed in the United States. Such transactions will be invalid as regards existing creditors who show that their debtor's financial condition was such as to justify the presumption that the donation would contribute to his insolvency.[1]

The statutory introduction of separate property rights for married women had a tendency to promote acts in fraud of creditors. Accordingly, in some cases, all dispositions between husband and wife have been subjected to special limitations.[2] Some statutes have also enacted positive restrictions upon gifts of the husband to the wife. The general provision is that such gifts shall not become the separate property of the wife.[3] Statutes, also, that have granted the married woman the right to hold the proceeds of insurance policies, drawn in her favor, upon the life of her husband, free from the claims of the latter's creditors, have frequently provided a maximum premium that may be paid

---

[1] Schouler, *H. & W.*, §§ 372-374.

[2] *Cf.* references *ante*, § 3.

[3] Col., An. St., 1891, § 3007; Kans., G. S., 1889, § 3752; Neb., C. S., 1891, § 1411; N. H., P. S., 1891, c. 176, § 1; Vt., Stat., 1894, § 2647; W. Va., Code, c. 66, § 3, as enacted by Acts, 1893, c. iii; Wy., R. S., 1887, § 1558. *Cf.* Del., Laws, vol. 15, c. 165, § 1, in R. C., 1893, p. 600; Md., Laws, 1898, c. 457, § 1. In Massachusetts, gifts between husband and wife are forbidden except that former may give latter articles of personal use not to exceed $2,000 in value. P. S., 1882, c. 147, § 3 as amended by Acts, 1884, c. 132. In the District of Columbia they become her separate property but are liable for the debts of the husband existing at the time the gift is made (Act, June 1, 1896, § 1, U. S. Stat. at Large, vol. 29, p. 193). Under former rule such gift did not become her separate property (Dist. of Col., R. S., 1873-74, § 727).

upon such policies. If the annual premium exceeds this amount the excess may be taken to satisfy the obligations of the husband.[4]

The European bankruptcy laws have followed the same principle in enabling creditors to attack gratuitous dispositions of the debtor in favor of his spouse where such transactions have been made within a limited period before the opening of the bankruptcy proceedings.[5] Moreover, by an application of the *praesumtio Muciana*, it is the general rule that the wife of the bankrupt must prove that property which she has acquired during the marriage, has not been purchased with her husband's money.[6]

A similar provision, primarily intended for the protection of creditors, raises the presumption that movables found in the possession of the husband[7] or, in some cases, of either of the married parties,[8] belong to the husband. In case community of property obtains, a general presumption is raised that existing goods belong to the common mass.[9] An

---

[4] *Cf. post*, § 38, note 27. N. Y., Laws, 1896, c. 272, § 22; Ohio, R. S., 1891, § 3628; Vt., Stat., 1894, §§ 2653-2657; W. Va., Code, 1891, c. 66, § 5, as amended by Acts, 1893, c. iii; Wis., An. St., 1889, § 2347 as amended by Laws, 1891, c. 376; Hawaii, C. L., 1884, p. 429; *cf.* Oklah., R. S., 1893, § 3080; Act 33 & 34 Vict., c. 93, § 10; Act 43 & 44 Vict., c. 26, § 2; Act 45 & 46 Vict., c. 75, § 11.

[5] Germany, *Kon. Ord.*, § 32, R. G. Bl., 1898, p. 619; Lehr, *Droit Russe*, pp. 42, 43; Leuthold, *R. R.*, p. 357; Alexander, *Konkursgesetze*, pp. 36, 127, 254, 492; *cf.* France, Code de Com., 564.

[6] Dig., 24, 1, 51; Germany, *Kon. Ord.*, § 45, R. G. Bl., 1898, p. 621; France, Code de Com., 557-562; Leuthold, *R. R.*, p. 357; Alexander, *Konkursgesetze*, p. 185; Dunscomb, *Bankruptcy*, p. 78.

[7] Saxony, B. G., § 1656; Norway, only as regards third parties, Stat. June 29, 1888, art. 21.

[8] Germany, only in favor of creditors, B. G., § 1362; Prussia, A. L. R., ii, 1, § 544; Russia, belong to the bankrupt, Lehr, *Droit Russe*, p. 43. *Cf.* Austria, B. G., § 1237; Nevada, G. S., 1885, §§ 501-503.

[9] Germany, B. G., § 1528; Prussia, A. L. R., ii, 1, §§ 400, 401. *Cf.* France, C. C., 1499; Italy, C. C., 1437; Spain, C. C., 1407; La., C. C., 2405.

exception arises respecting things intended for the personal
use of the wife.[10] For such objects the German code raises
the presumption of the wife's ownership, not only as between
the parties, but also as regards creditors.[11]

Donations, which do not affect the rights of third parties,
may, nevertheless, be restricted as between the parties themselves. The chief cause for such limitations has been the consideration that one of the parties, under the strong influences
arising from the conjugal relation, may be led to make
extravagant and unreasonable benefits for the other party,
Another motive has been the principle that in the true marriage everything should be for the common benefit. To
permit gifts would be to introduce a selfish element which
would injuriously affect the ideal unity established by the
marriage.

The Roman law prohibited gifts between married parties.
It was probably influenced by considerations of the community of interests established by the union of the parties, but
the chief basis of the rule, as it is recognized in the law of
Justinian, is the desire to protect married parties against the
undue influences connected with the intimate relation into
which they have entered.[12] This consideration receives
additional force as a result of the existence of the Roman
institution of free divorce. In the absence of restrictions
upon donations, it would have been possible for an unscru-
pulous spouse to obtain benefits as a result of the affection
and confidence of the other, and then, by exercising the
right of divorce, leave such party despoiled and helpless.

There were many exceptions to the general rule of Roman
law that donations between husband and wife are invalid.
Thus, it was recognized that gifts of articles for personal use

[10] Germany, B. G., § 1362; Saxony, B. G., § 1656; Norway, Stat. June 29,
1888, art. 22; Russia, Lehr, *Droit Russe*, p. 43.

[11] B. G., § 1362.   [12] Dig., 24, 1, 1 *seq.*

or those made on customary occasions are valid.[13] Moreover, the act of donation is not void, but voidable at the option of the donor, and if he dies without having demanded the return of the gift the title of the donee cannot be impeached.[14]

The early German law imposed no restrictions upon gifts between married parties, but such transactions were effective only to the extent that the wife's individual title to property was recognized.[15] Some of the modern legislations, however, have recognized the rule of Roman law.[16] The French civil code reaches the same end in a slightly different manner. Donations between husband and wife are permitted, under certain restrictions as to amount,[17] but they are always revocable by the donor, and, for such revocation, the married woman does not require the marital authorization.[18] In some of the states the general regulations governing contracts between married parties will restrict acts of donation between them.[19]

The rule of German law has been followed in other states, and gifts between husband and wife are determined by the same principles as obtain for donations between strangers.[20] The fiction of unity in the English common law prevented gifts as well as other transactions between married

---

[13] Windscheid, *Pandekten*, vol. ii, § 509.   [14] *Ibid.*

[15] Schröder, *Lehrbuch*, pp. 728, 729.

[16] Italy, C. C., 1054; Spain, C. C., 1334, 1335; Saxony, B. G., §§ 1647, 1649, 1694; Finland, Stat. Apl. 15, 1889, c. iii, art. 6. In Norway donations to be valid must be made by marriage contract, unless they consist in objects for personal use or life insurance policies or annuities. Stat. June 29, 1888, art. 24.

[17] France, C. C., 1094, 1098.   [18] *Ibid.*, 1096.

[19] *Cf.* references, *ante*, § 3.

[20] Austria, B. G., § 1246; Prussia, A. L. R., ii, 1, §§ 310, 311; Russia, Leuthold, *R. R.*, pp. 59, 60. No particular restrictions are placed upon donations between married parties in the code of Germany, and hence the above rule obtains in this system.

parties. In equity, however, where this fiction is not recognized, such acts will be sustained if the gift has passed from one into the possession of the other.[21] Executed gifts cannot generally be revoked except under circumstances which would justify a revocation between strangers, but the court will more readily impute fraud or mistake in gifts from wife to husband than in ordinary cases.[22] The provisions of the married women's acts, that gifts from the husband to the wife shall not become her separate property,[23] while primarily established in the interests of third parties, will affect the transactions as between the parties themselves. The husband's common law rights attach to the objects, and, if the latter consist of personal property, the husband may regain full ownership in the same.

§ 6. *The Married Woman as a Trader.*

The legal capacity of the married woman has been influenced also by the increased activity of women in industrial and commercial spheres. The majority of the legislations provide means whereby she can undertake a trade or business in her own name and on her own account. But in some European countries, the interests of the conjugal society as well as the system of matrimonial property relations have led to the requirement that the consent of the husband shall be necessary to the exercise of such functions.[1] In Germany, the principle of the general capacity of married women enables them to carry on business even if the husband refuses his

---

[21] Schouler, *H. & W.*, §383.   [22] *Ibid.*, § 390.

[23] See references, *ante*, note 3.

[1] France, Code de Com., 4; Prussia, A. L. R., ii, 1, §195; Saxony, B. G., § 1638. Tacit consent is sufficient: Germany, B. G., §§ 1405, 1452, 1519, 1549; Switzerland, Federal Law of Obligations, art. 35, *An. étran.*, vol. 11, p. 525. In Austria this consent will be supplied by the court if such activity will not endanger the rights of the husband; Stat. Dec. 17, 1862, R. G. Bl, 1863, pp. 1, 2; *cf.* general power of court to supply marital authorization, *ante*, § 3.

consent, but, in case his objections have been publicly made known,[2] the acts of the wife will bind only her separate property. If the business requires personal service upon the part of the wife, the husband will be able to cause its cessation by appeal to the court.[3]

Even before the passage of the married women's statutes, the English and American courts had recognized the wife's right, under certain conditions, to carry on a trade or business. The husband was entitled to his wife's services, but he could make her a gift of the same so far as such act did not violate the rules against donations in fraud of creditors.[4] Where the married woman possessed a separate estate she could contract with reference to the same, and was entitled to the profits accruing therefrom.[5] This did not include, however, the proceeds arising from the personal management of a trade or business. The latter were connected with the personal industry of the wife, and hence the consent of the husband was an essential element, though such consent might be implied, at least as between the parties themselves.[6]

Under the married women's acts, the wife, so far as she has been granted general contractual capacity, may carry on a trade or business. This right has been limited in certain systems. In some of the states it is restricted to undertakings carried on for the support of the married woman and those dependent upon her, where the husband fails to provide such support.[7] The authorization of the court or public notice or both are sometimes required.[8]

[2] B. G., §§ 1405, 1435.   [3] *Ibid.* §1358; *cf. ante,* § 3.   [4] See *ante,* § 5.
[5] See *ante,* § 3, note 48.   [6] Schouler, *H. & W.,* § 302 *seq.*
[7] Idaho, R. S., 1887, § 5850 *seq.;* Mont., C. C. P., 1895, § 2290 *seq.;* Nev. G. S., 1885, § 534 *seq.;* Wis., An. St., 1889, § 2344; *cf.* W. Va., Acts, 1893, c. iii, § 14.
[8] Idaho, see preceding note; Mont., *ibid.;* Nev., *ibid.;* Fla., R. S., 1885, §1505 *seq.;* Mass., Acts, 1898, c. 416; in North Carolina, the written consent of the husband is required, Code, 1883, § 1827 *seq.*

While the legislations differ with respect to the conditions under which the married woman may acquire the right to carry on a trade or business, there is general agreement that the capacity, when once acquired, is as extensive as that possessed by an unmarried woman. The disabilities and privileges of the wife do not apply to married women traders.[9]

§ 7. *The Married Woman's Capacity to Sue and be Sued.*

The circumstances which produced restrictions upon the contractual capacity of the married woman led to limitations upon her power to conduct a judicial proceeding. The Roman law and modern legislations, in the practical elimination of sex as a basis of private legal capacity, and the creation of separate property rights for the married woman, have removed the chief conditions which gave occasion for such restrictions. Hence, the tendency has been to grant the married woman the general capacity to sue and be sued, subject to qualifications with respect to particular matters.

The limitations which continue to exist are justified, in general, by considerations of domestic unity and harmony and of the preservation of the matrimonial property relations. These considerations, as well as a survival of the conception of the natural incapacity of the sex, affect the provisions of the French code and of those statutes that have been largely influenced by it. The married woman is subjected in this capacity to the same general restrictions that are imposed upon her power of contracting obligations. The marital authorization must be obtained before the wife

---

[9] Germany, B. G., § 1405; France, Code de Com., 5, but a married woman, even if a trader, cannot plead in her own name without marital authorization, C. C., 215; Switzerland, Federal Law of Obligations, art. 35, *An. étran.*, vol. 11, p. 525; Louisiana, C. C., 1786; Leuthold, *R. R.*, p. 199; *cf.* Windscheid, *Pandekten*, vol. ii, §§ 486–488; Schouler, *H. & W.*, § 310.

can become a party to a civil proceeding.[1]   In all cases she
may appeal to the court from the husband's refusal to grant
his consent.[2]   Moreover, the marital authorization is not
required for legal proceedings which the wife undertakes for
the protection of her property against the husband.[3]

The states which accept the principle that the general
capacity of the woman is not affected by the marriage,
recognize the right of the wife to carry on judicial proceedings.   The interests of the husband are safeguarded by the
provision that such acts will not be binding upon the
matrimonial property unless his consent or joinder has been
obtained.[4]

At English common law the married woman cannot undertake an independent suit at law.   In all cases, except
where she has acquired the position of a *femme sole* by
reason of the civil disabilities of her husband, she must join
with the latter in such a proceeding.   In courts of equity
the opposition of interests between husband and wife is recognized.   This does not invest the latter with the capacity
of conducting legal proceedings, and hence she must always
be represented by a trustee or next friend.

The acts creating a statutory separate estate for married
women generally carried with them an express or implied
grant of capacity to carry on legal proceedings with refer-

[1] France, C. C., 215; Italy, C. C., 134; Spain, C. C., 60; La., C. C., 125.

[2] France, C. C., 218, 219, 222, C. C. P., 861, 862; Italy, C. C., 136; Spain, C. C., 60; La., C. C., 124, 132.

[3] France, C. C., 1443, 1563; Italy, C. C., 1418, 1442; Spain, C. C., 60; La., C. C., 2391, 2425.

[4] Germany, *Civilprozessordnung*, § 52, R. G. Bl., 1898, p. 419, B. G., § 1400. In the interests of domestic harmony, the wife is not permitted to proceed against the husband for claims arising out of his administration of the matrimonial prop-erty until after the end of such administration. This does not prevent her from taking measures for the security of her property, B. G., § 1394; Austria, *Civil-prozessordnung*, § 1, R. G. Bl., 1895, p. 365; *cf.* Prussia, A. L. R., ii, 1, §§ 189, 230; Saxony, B. G., § 1638; Finland, Stat. Apl. 15, 1889, c. ii, arts. 3, 5.

ence to the same. The legislation upon the subject is not uniform and its scope has not been fully determined. Some of the states limit the capacity to matters affecting the separate estate of the married woman, while others extend it to proceedings affecting her person or character. In a few legislations, positive enactments require the joinder of the husband in suits to which the wife is a party, while some permit and others prohibit such joinder. Despite the particular differences, a general tendency may be noted to accord the married woman full capacity in this respect, wherever it will not affect the matrimonial property rights accorded to the husband. Most of the states have established the system of separate property between married parties, and in these states the wife is generally permitted to sue and be sued in all matters as a *femme sole*.[5] A few states recognize the desirability of preserving the domestic unity from contentious proceedings by prohibiting suits between husband and wife, while others, in permitting such suits as regards property, forbid either party to sue the other for a tort.

A feature of interest in this connection is the fact that special privileges which were accorded to the wife on account of her incapacity to sue, have not always been repealed with the removal of such disability. Following an old English statute, most of the states granted the married woman an immunity from the effects of statutes providing for the limitations of actions. The running of the period of limitation was suspended during coverture. The acts granting the married woman capacity to carry on legal proceedings did not generally provide for the repeal of such privileges. Where the statute provided that the running of the period of limitations should be suspended until after the dis-

---

[5] See references to English and American statutes, *ante*, § 3.

abilities of coverture were removed, it would seem that its provisions could not be taken advantage of by a married woman who has complete capacity for carrying on legal actions. The later revisions of statutes show a tendency to eliminate the provisions granting these privileges to married women.

§ 8. *Right and Duty of Household Administration.*

All countries recognize the marriage as establishing a community of life between the married parties. It is also the rule that the husband is the head of the family and has the right of determining respecting the affairs of the family household, the wife being under a general obligation to assist him in such administration. The question arises respecting the extent to which the wife has a right as well as a duty of acting within the field of household affairs. The question is affected by the distribution of the burden of the family expenses. Where these are primarily or exclusively supported by the husband, the wife's right of administration is subjected to marital authorization or entirely excluded. If the wife assists in bearing these expenses she is generally recognized as having a certain right of administration.

Some European legislations recognize the right of the wife to act in matters pertaining to the ordinary support of the family. This is based upon the principle that she is acting as the agent of the husband, and hence, where the latter manifests a contrary desire, this capacity of the wife will be excluded.[1]

The English common law followed a similar principle in permitting the married woman to contract for necessities

[1] Where this principle is not recognized in positive statutes, it will generally be supplied by the courts. In Spain it does not appear that the husband can deprive the wife of such.right. See also, Basle, Stat. Mch. 10, 1884, arts. 7, 34; Finland, Stat. Apl. 15, 1889, c. iv, art. 2.

upon the credit of her husband.[2] If the presumption of
agency is contradicted by positive statements of the husband
or by the fact that he has furnished sufficient necessaries for
the support of the family, he will not be liable for such contracts of his wife. A tendency has appeared to make the
rule more favorable for the wife. If the husband does not
provide the necessities, third parties may furnish them to
the wife despite the prohibition of the husband.[3]

In Germany and some of the Swiss cantons the married
woman is accorded a more extensive right of household
administration. Thus, the wife's acts of customary household management, even though concluded without the marital authorization, will be binding upon the husband. In
some of the older legislations it is recognized that the husband can relieve himself from this obligation for the future
by a public declaration, before the court, that the wife shall
not possess such authority.[4] The new German code and
the draft code of Switzerland give the wife a positive right
of household administration.[5] The former permits the husband to limit or exclude this function of the wife, but the
court may reinstate her in such capacity if it considers that
the husband has abused his power. The draft code of
Switzerland, following the Lucerne statute of November 26,
1880, goes a step further than the German code. It considers the married woman as having full capacity of household administration until she has been deprived of the same
by judicial decree.[6] This position meets the demands of

---

[2] Blackstone, *Comm.*, vol. i, p. 442; Pol. & Mait., *Hist.*, vol. ii, p. 402.

[3] Kent, *Comm.*, vol. ii, p. 149; *cf.* La., C. C., 1786; Hawaii, Laws, 1888, c. xi, § 7.

[4] Prussia, A. L. R., ii, 1, § 323; Glaris, L. B., ii, art. 175; Zürich, P. R. G., § 603;
in Saxony the declaration must be known to the third party, B. G., §§ 1645, 1699.

[5] Germany, B. G., §§ 1356, 1357; Switz., *Vorentwurf*, 180, 182; a statute of
November 26, 1880, art. 15, established the same principle in the canton of
Lucerne (*An. étran*, vol. 10, p. 488).

[6] Switz., *Vorentwurf*, 183; Lucerne, Stat. Nov. 26, 1880, art. 15.

the representatives of the German society "Frauenwohl." [7]
The "Rechtsschützverein für Frauen," in Dresden, insists,
however, that each party shall have equal capacity of household administration, and shall bind the other to the extent
that the latter has not renounced such liability by public
declaration before the court. [8]

[7] Sera Proelsz und Marie Raschke: *Die Frau im neuen bürgerlichen Gesetzbuch.*

[8] See *Das deutsche Recht und die deutschen Frauen*, p. 7.

PART II.

MATRIMONIAL PROPERTY SYSTEMS.

CHAPTER I.

CLASSIFICATION.

§ 9. *In General.*

AT first glance the different classes of matrimonial property systems appear innumerable. The local customs which continued to govern the family relations in Europe after the reception of Roman law, were developed into a multitude of particular systems. But the modern codification movement has brought about a greater degree of uniformity. It is clear, moreover, that underneath the differences occasioned by the accidental circumstances attending their growth, many of the systems have essential features in common.

The question of title or ownership, which is the most essential element in any kind of property relations, furnishes the most fundamental basis for a classification of matrimonial property systems. Accepting this as a principle, the numberless particular regimes may be grouped under the two general divisions of communal and individual systems. The first class includes all the systems which recognize common ownership of any general part of the property of the married parties, while all other systems fall under the second division.

The value of the above classification is not affected by the fact that under an individual system the husband and wife may hold property in common. Particular instances of common ownership do not determine the general character of the system. If, however, the communal principle is applied to any general part of the property of either of the parties, the system must be distinguished from those falling under the individual class, notwithstanding that the parties may hold property by individual title.

The systems grouped under one of these two divisions, possess in common the characteristic feature which distinguishes them from those falling under the other class. Within each division, however, fundamental differences among the systems furnish the basis for further classification.

§ 10. *Communal Systems.*

The most natural basis for classifying communal systems is to be found in the extent or scope of the principle of community. Upon such basis two divisions may be formed. The general community of property (*allgemeine Gütergemeinschaft; communauté universelle*) embraces all systems in which the principle of common ownership is applied to the entire fortune of each of the married parties. Limited or particular community includes those communal systems in which a general class of property is excluded from the common ownership.

The number of forms of limited community is restricted only by the capacity to develop new modifications of the communal principle; but, as they have been defined in the important legislations, they fall under the classes of community of acquisitions (*Errungenschaftsgemeinschaft; communauté réduite aux acquêts*) or community of movables and acquisitions (*Fahrnissgemeinschaft*). Under the former the ownership of the individual property which either party possesses at the beginning of the community is not affected, but the income and profits of such property and, in general, everything that is acquired by either party during the existence of the community, becomes common property. The system of community of movables and acquisitions is the same as the above, except that the ownership of the movables which either party possesses, at the beginning of the community, becomes common.

Some of the other principal types of limited community are indicated in the civil code of France.[1] They are characterized by the provisions for partial or complete exclusion of movables; inclusion of immovables by fictitiously treating them as movables; exclusion of ante-nuptial debts; exclusion of objects gratuitously acquired; a privilege for the wife of resuming her contributions without loss at the close of the community; special privileges for the survivor, and for unequal shares in the community.

§ 11. *Individual Systems.*

These systems do not differ among themselves with reference to the application of the principle of individual ownership. The property, in general, under all of such systems, continues to be held by individual title. The individual property systems, however, differ among themselves respecting the nature and extent of the interest which either party, by virtue of the marriage, acquires in the property of the other. In accordance with this test four subdivisions of this group may be obtained:

I. System of Exclusive Rights of the Husband;

The husband is entitled to the complete control and, aside from exceptions arising from peculiar circumstances, to the ownership of the property of the wife. The individual title of the wife is transferred to the husband.

[1] France, C. C., 1497 *seq.*

II. System of Marital Administration and Usufruct;

The husband has the administration and is entitled to the fruits and profits of the property of the wife. The latter, however, retains the individual ownership of her property.

III. System of Dowry;

The marriage does not affect the property of the parties, but it is customary for the husband to receive a contribution to assist him in supporting the expenses of the common household. He does not acquire an absolute title, but he has the right of administration over the dowry, and is entitled to the proceeds arising from the same.

IV. System of Separate Property;

Neither party acquires, by virtue of the marriage, any right or interest in the property of the other. The title and the use and administration of the fortune of each party remains unaffected by the marriage.

CHAPTER II.

REGULATION BY MARRIAGE AGREEMENTS.

§ 12. *General Freedom to contract such Agreements.*

The capacity of the parties to determine the property relations that shall exist between them is a consideration of fundamental importance, Two opposing principles appear in this connection. On one hand there is the desirability of uniformity, particularly in the interests of third parties. On the other hand, there is presented the great value of allowing free scope to individual traits and wishes in this field of human relationships. Any determination which is made of this question will be influenced by both of these considerations.

In considering the attitude of the states respecting marriage agreements, it will be necessary to distinguish between those which are concluded before the marriage and those which are entered into after the relation has been established. All of the important states permit the regulation of matrimonial property relations by ante-nuptial agreements between the parties.[1] The legal disabilities resulting from the marriage do not attach until the relation has been

---

[1] Many of the Swiss cantons do not permit the matrimonial property relations to be regulated by agreement of the parties. Alterations of the statutory system can obtain only to the extent that they have the effect of contracts of inheritance. In certain cases the court is authorized to approve alterations for specific reasons. For chart showing attitude of cantons respecting marriage contracts see Lardy, *Législations Suisses*, Appendix; see also, Lucerne, Stat. Nov. 26, 1880, art. 27; Zürich, P. R. G., §§ 615–619. The draft code of Switzerland permits the parties to determine their legal property relations by contract, *Vorentwurf*, 195.

entered upon. Prior to that time the parties may make any contract respecting property that may be made between strangers. This general rule is subject to particular exceptions which will be considered in a subsequent section. [2]

The widespread acceptance of the above principle indicates its essential value, It is at once an indication of the difficulty of defining a perfect system, and a recognition of the necessity of affording considerable freedom to the influence of local customs and individual characteristics in the field of matrimonial relations.

These general considerations have not, however, received full application in all cases. A distinction is made in some systems between ante-nuptial and post-nuptial agreements. Particular considerations are involved in the case of contracts concluded after marriage, hence such agreements may be subjected to restrictions or absolutely prohibited. The grounds for such departure from the general principle are for the most part the same as those previously considered as the basis for restrictions upon general transactions between husband and wife.[3] Fear exists that one of the parties will use his influence over the other for selfish advantage, or it is desired to protect third parties against collusive acts of married parties.

The Civil Code of France and those systems that have adopted its provisions or have been strongly influenced by it,[4] generally provide that after the marriage ceremony has been performed, a contract regulating the property relations of the parties cannot be entered into, and that an ante-nuptial contract cannot be altered or modified by any sub-

[2] *Post*, § 14.

[3] See *ante*, §§ 3–5.

[4] France, C. C., 1395, 1543; Italy, C. C., 1385, 1391; Spain, C. C., 1320; Finland, Stat. Apl. 15, 1889, c. iii, art. 6; Basle, Stat. Mch. 10, 1884, art. 17; Ariz., R. S., 1887, § 2099; La., C. C., 2329; Texas, R. S., 1895, art. 2965.

sequent agreement.[5]   To the extent that the American systems have retained the common law prohibition upon contracts between husband and wife, the same rule obtains.[6]

On the other hand, those systems that impose no general limitations upon contracts between husband and wife permit the regulation or modification of matrimonial property relations by post-nuptial agreements between the parties.[7]

§ 13. *Statutory and Contractual Systems.*

As a rule the states of continental Europe, in addition to determining the property relations that shall obtain between the husband and wife, where they have failed to enter into a marriage agreement *(gesetzliches Güterrecht; régime légal)*, make provision in the codes for one or more systems that may become operative as a result of a contract between the parties *(vertragsmässiges Güterrecht; régime conventionnel)*. The immediate occasion for the existence of such provisions was the condition of the law regulating matrimonial property relations before the adoption of the modern codes.   Within a single state, a large number of different systems obtained by force of local customs or statutes. This condition may be explained on one hand as the result of feudal decentralization, and on the other by the greater resistance to the reception of Roman law in the field of

---

[5] A general exception permits the parties to re-establish community of property which may have been dissolved by separation of goods.   France, C. C., 1451; Italy, C. C., 1443; Spain, C. C., 1320; Finland, Stat. Apl. 15, 1889, c. v, art. 17.

[6] *Cf.* references *ante*, § 3.

[7] Austria, B. G., § 1217; Germany, B. G., 1432; Prussia, A. L. R., ii, 1, §§ 215, 251, 355, 412, 419, 439, but exceptions arise where the contract establishes community of goods or where it provides for the exclusion of such community in districts where the latter exists by force of local statutes, though community existing as a result of contract may be dissolved or modified by post-nuptial agreement, *ibid.*, ii, 1, §§ 354 *seq.*, 412 *seq.;* Saxony, B. G., § 1691; Norway, Stat. June 29, 1888, arts. 3, 4; Leuthold, *R. R.*, pp. 59, 60; *cf.* references to English and American statutes, *ante*, § 3.

family relations. In Germany, before the adoption of the present code, more than one hundred matrimonial property systems were given statutory recognition.[1] Similar conditions had existed in other European states before the nationalization of the law was accomplished. While the variations in some cases were of slight importance, in other cases the differences among the systems were fundamental.

It was recognized that a sharp break with the old customs and legislations would produce hardships, and that mere freedom of contract would not be sufficient to overcome this condition so far as the mass of the population was concerned. Individuals, who desired a system differing from that established by the code, would be obliged to set forth in detail the terms under which they desired to have their property relations regulated. A failure to express themselves clearly might frequently lead to results the reverse of those desired. The German code commissioners considered various plans for the solution of this difficulty. One proposal was that the local customs and statutes should be continued in the field of matrimonial property relations. This policy had been followed by Prussia and other German states as they absorbed neighboring communities, and by Russia with respect to Finland and other Swedish and Polish provinces.[2] Another plan proposed to divide Germany into districts and establish for each district, as a statutory system, that which obtained among the majority of the people within such territory. It was also proposed that the legislative authority of each commonwealth should be permitted to determine which of several systems defined by the federal code, should obtain within its jurisdiction.[3]

[1] *Denkschrift*, p. 450.   *Cf.* Neubauer, *Deutschland.*

[2] Neubauer, *Deutschland*, pp. 1 *seq.*, 66, 209 *seq.*, 228, 231, 233, 240; Neubauer, *Ausland*, pp. 22–24.

[3] Gierke, *Entwurf*, p. 111 *seq.;* Bähr, " Das eheliche Güterrecht des bürgerlichen Gesetzbuchs," *Arch. f. bürg. Recht.*, vol. i, p. 237.

These proposals met with serious objections on the ground of the practical difficulties as well as from considerations of the interests of national unity.[4] They have not been accepted in the more modern codes which undertake to remove the inconveniences arising from the establishment of a single statutory system by giving legal definition to several systems. One of these, probably that which obtains among the greater number of people or which corresponds most closely to their social ideas and institutions, is established as the statutory system. It comes into operation, however, only in so far as the married parties have failed to indicate a different desire.[5] Any one of the other systems may be introduced by marriage contract. The simple indication of the title of the system will be sufficient to bring its provisions into operation. In this way the freedom of contract is made much more effective.

The beneficial character of this policy is manifested by the widespread acceptance which it has received. The following table indicates the statutory and contractual systems that have been defined in the legislations which have been brought under consideration in the present study :[6]

[4] *Motive*, vol. iv, p. 133; *Denkschrift*, pp. 270, 271; Mitteis, " Bemerkungen zum ehelichen Güterrecht," *Zeit. f. d. privat. u. öff. Rechts.*, vol. 16, p. 562.

[5] In a certain sense two statutory systems exist in legislations which recognize a legal or judicial separation of property in case of community of goods, marital administration and usufruct or dowry. Where such separation occurs, the regime of separate property becomes the matrimonial property system by operation of law. *Post*, §§ 24, 31, 36.

[6] The codes which recognize the system of dowry practically define the system of separate property in providing for the constitution and administration of the paraphernalia. *Post*, §32.

Code or Statute.	*Statutory System.*	*Contractual Systems.*
France, C. C.[7]	Community of Movables and Acquisitions (art. 1393).	General Community, Community of Acquisitions, and six other forms of Limited Community (art. 1497 *seq.*); Marital Administration and Usufruct (art. 1529 *seq.*); Dowry (art. 1540 *seq.*); Separate property (art. 1536 *seq.*).[8]
Spain, C. C.	Community of Acquisitions (art. 1315).	Dowry (art. 1336).
Italy, C. C.	Dowry (art. 1388 *seq.*).	Community of Acquisitions (art. 1438).
Austria, B. G.	Dowry (§1218).[9]	General and Limited Community of Property (§ 1233 *seq.*).
Basle City (Stat. Mch. 10, 1884).	General Community (art. 1).	Separate Property (arts. 1, 28).
Geneva, C. C.	Same as France, C. C.	Same as France, C. C.
Glaris, L. B	Marital Administration and Usufruct (ii, arts. 172, 173).	
Lucerne, Stat. Nov. 26, 1880.	Marital Administration and Usufruct (art. 4 *seq.*).	
Zürich, P. R. G.[10]	Marital Administration and Usufruct (§ 589 *seq.*).	
Switzerland, Vorentwurf[11]	Marital Administration and Usufruct (art. 196).	General Community (art. 244 *seq.*); Community of Movables and Acquisitions (arts. 264, 265); Community of Acquisitions (arts. 266, 267); Separate Property (art. 268 *seq.*).

[7] The provisions of the French Civil Code, or their substantial equivalent, obtain in Belgium and Geneva and before the adoption of the German code, were in force in Baden, Elsass-Lothringen and in districts of Prussia, Bavaria, Hesse, *etc.*

[8] During the Middle Ages the community of acquisitions was in some places combined with the system of dowry, the profits of the dowry falling into the community (Viollet, *Précis*, p. 689). This composite system is recognized as a contractual system in France (C. C., 1581) and Italy (C. C., 1433), and will arise in Spain (C. C., 1315) and Louisiana (C. C., 2399) whenever dowry is established and no contrary provision is made.

[9] Before the adoption of the German code, the system of dowry obtained in the territory of the common or Roman law to the extent that the latter had not been altered by statute. *Cf. Denkschrift*, p. 450.

[10] Among the other Swiss cantons are to be found, in addition to those above indicated, the systems of community of acquisitions and of dowry. *Cf.* Neubauer, *Ausland*, pp. 1–7.

[11] The central government has been given the power to establish a uniform code of private law. So far as concerns family law and the law of persons, the action has not passed the initiatory stage.

Germany, B. G...............Marital Administration and Usufruct (§ 1363 *seq.*). General Community (§ 1437 *seq.*); Community of Movables and Acquisitions (§ 1549 *seq.*); Community of Acquisitions (§ 1437 *seq.*); Separate property (§§ 1436, 1426 *seq.*).

Prussia, A. L. R. ....Marital Administration and Usufruct (ii, 1, § 205) [12] General Community (ii, 1,§ 360); Community of Acquisitions (ii, 1, § 396); Separate Property (ii, 1, §§ 208, 221 *seq.*).

Saxony, B. G................Marital Administration and Usufruct (§ 1655). General Community (§ 1695); Limited Community (§ 1703); Separate Property (§ 1693).

Norway, Stat. June 29, 1888 [13]..General Community, Separate Property.
Finland, Stat. Apl. 15, 1889.....Community of Movables and Acquisitions (C. i, art. 1 *seq.*).

Russia [14].....................Separate Property.

England [15] ....Separate Property.

United States of America.[15] All legislations except those indicated below.[16] . ...Separate Property.

Arizona, R. S., 1887 ....Community of Acquisitions (§ 2102).

California, C. C...............Community of Acquisitions (§ 164).

Idaho, R. S., 1887.............Community of Acquisitions (§ 2497).

Louisiana, C. C. ....Community of Acquisitions (art. 2332). Dowry (art. 2335 *seq.*),

Nevada, G. S., 1888...........Community of Acquisitions (§ 500).

New Mexico, C. L., 1897 [17] ....Community of Acquisitions (§ 2030 *seq.*).

Texas, R. S., 1895 ....Community of Acquisitions (art. 2968).

Washington, G. S., 1891.......Community of Acquisitions (§ 1399).

---

[12] Where provincial statutes established community as the statutory system the system of marital administration and usufruct became a contractual system.

[13] Denmark recognizes general community, while in Sweden community is limited to movables and acquisitions. Neubauer, *Ausland*, p. 22.

[14] Within the jurisdiction of the civil code. Lehr, *Droit Russe*, p. 42; Leuthold *R. R.*, p. 59.

[15] For English and American statutes, see references *post*, § 38.

[16] For particular exceptions in Florida and Tennessee, see *post*, § 38.

[17] *Cf. post*, § 17 (b), note 6.

The parties in accepting the statutory system or any of the contractual systems may, in general, introduce such modifications as they desire.[18] It will thus be a relatively easy matter to transform general community into a limited community, and either of these, as well as marital administration and usufruct, into a condition of separate property, even if such forms are not given statutory definition as contractual systems.

To guard against confusion and indefiniteness the parties are forbidden to provide in general terms for the regulation of their property relations by local customs or foreign laws. They must accept one of the systems defined in the code, or set forth in detail the rules according to which they desire their economic interests to be governed.[19]

§ 14. *Particular Provisions Respecting Marriage Contracts.*

The exercise of the general right of determining matrimonial property relations by contract is subject to certain conditions imposed in the interest of the family or of third parties. A common provision is the requirement of special forms in marriage agreements. It is very generally the rule that the agreement shall be reduced to writing and signed by the parties. This principle was established in English law, so far as regards executory agreements, by the fourth section

[18] In Finland the system of separate property cannot be introduced by contract. Stat. Apl. 15, 1889, c. i, art. 4; in Germany the provisions respecting the continuation of the community between the survivor and the common children may be excluded, but cannot be otherwise altered in any manner. B. G., §§ 1508, 1518; in Italy the parties are forbidden to contract for any community other than that of acquisitions. C. C., 1433, *cf. ibid.*, 1434–1436; for limitations in Swiss cantons, see *ante*, § 12, note 1.

[19] France, C. C., 1390; Italy, C. C., 1381; Spain, C. C., 1317; Germany, an exception arises in case the husband is residing in a foreign country at the time the contract is concluded. B. G., § 1433.

of the famous Statute of Frauds.[1] It obtains in practically
all of the states of the American union.

Most of the continental European legislations and some of
the American statutes go further and require that the contract shall be drawn up before a notary or judge.[2] Wit-
nesses are generally necessary and, in some cases, the act
must receive judicial confirmation.

In addition, it is provided in many states that marriage
agreements shall receive official publication or registration.[3]
The code of Germany has established a special matrimonial
property register for such publication, and the draft code of
Switzerland proposes a similar record.[4] These requirements
exist in the interest of third parties, and a failure to observe
them will not generally affect the rights of the parties as
between themselves.

A limitation upon the right of the parties to affect their
mutual property relations sometimes occurs in connection
with dispositions to take effect upon the death of one of the
parties. Some legislations provide that marriage contracts

<hr>

[1] Act 29 Car. ii, c. 3.

[2] France, C. C., 1394 *seq.*; Italy, C. C., 1382 *seq.*; Spain, C. C., 1321 *seq.*;
Austria, Stat. July 25, 1871, R. G. Bl., no. 76; Germany, B. G., § 1434; Prussia,
A. L. R., ii, 1, §§ 198, 209, 356; Basle, Stat. Mch. 10, 1884, art. 17; Switz.,
Vorentwurf, 219, 220; Ariz., R. S., 1887, § 2098; La., C. C., 2328 *seq.*; Texas,
R. S., 1895, art. 2964; Wash., G. S., 1891, § 1401.

[3] Italy, C. C., 1384; Germany, B. G., § 1435; Prussia, in case of exclusion of
community, A. L. R., ii, 1, § 422; Saxony, B. G., § 1695; Norway, Stat. June 29,
1888, art. 2 *seq.*; Finland, Stat. Apl. 15, 1889, c. iii, art. 1 *seq.*; Switz., *Vorentwurf*, 222 *seq.*; Ala., Code, 1896, § 1011; Ark., Dig. Stat. 1894, §§ 4898–4901;
Cal., C. C., §§ 178–180; Geo., Code, 1895, § 2483; Idaho, R. S., 1887, §§ 2508–
2511; Ill., An. St., 1885, c. 68, ¶9; Ky., Stat. 1894, § 2128; Mass., P. S., 1882,
c. 147, § 2; Miss., An. Code, 1892, § 2294; Mo., R. S., 1889, §§ 6853, 6854;
Mont., C. C., 1885, §§ 248–250; Nev., G. S., 1885, §§ 524–528; N. C., Code,
1883, §§ 1270, 1820, 1821; S. C., C. S. L., 1893, § 2168; Tenn., Code, 1884,
§§ 2837, 2846; Hawaii, C. L., 1884, § 1263; so far as either party is a trader:
Austria, R. G. Bl., 1863, pp. 3, 4; France, Code de Com., 67 *seq.*

[4] Germany, B. G., §§ 1558–1563; Switz., *Vorentwurf*, 222–225.

shall not affect the rights of the survivor nor change the legal order of succession.[5]   Where the principle of the legal portion is recognized, the parties will generally be unable to modify the same either as regards themselves or their heirs.[6]

[5] France, C. C., 1388, 1389, 1527; Italy, C. C., 1379, 1380, 1398; Ariz., R. S., 1887, § 2097; La., C. C., 2326; Texas, R. S., 1895, art. 2963; *cf.* Switz., *Vorentwurf*, 221.

[6] *Post*, § 47.

CHAPTER III.

SYSTEMS OF COMMUNITY OF PROPERTY.

§ 15. *Common, Dotal and Separate Property.*

In considering the systems which recognize common property of married parties, it is necessary to distinguish three classes of property. Theoretically it would appear that the system of general community embraces only one kind of property, while limited community implies the existence of only two classes. In practice, however, most of the legislations define three distinct species under all kinds of community, and the freedom of contract tends to promote this division. These three classes may be characterized as common, dotal and separate property.[1]

Common property includes all objects that fall into the common mass. It is held by the married parties in joint ownership, each of them having a right to an indivisible share of the whole. The profits and proceeds accruing from such property likewise belong to the common fund.

Property which is excluded from joint ownership and is held by individual title by either married party is either dotal or separate in character. These terms are chosen in the absence of more definite legal expressions. The codes, while recognizing the difference between the two kinds of property, generally include both under the class of property

---

[1] The two latter classes, and, in particular instances, the first class also, will appear under individual as well as in communal systems. See *post*, chap. iv.

reserved from community (*Vorbehaltsgut ;* biens réservés).
The first draft of the German code used the terms, "Son
dergut" and "Vorbehaltsgut," to distinguish the two
classes.[3] The later drafts omitted the former term, and no
particular expression was adopted for the characterization
of such property under the system of general community,[4]
though the term, "eingebrachtes Gut" is applied to it
under the systems of limited community.[5]

Dotal and separate property agree in that each is held by
an individual title, but they differ with respect to administration and usufruct. Dotal property is administered for
the benefit of both parties, and the profits and proceeds become common property.[6] It differs from the latter only in
the fact that the exclusive title of the individual owner is retained, and hence the capital of the property does not form
a part of the common mass.[7]

Separate property, on the other hand, continues subject
to individual administration and usufruct according to the
general principles obtaining for the system of separate
property.

§ 16. *Composition of the General Community.*

The general community of all property has been advo-
cated as the only system that realizes the ideal of the mar-

[2] Under the systems of marital administration and usufruct as well as of dowry, the two classes are clearly distinguished by the terms, " dotal property " and " re-served property " or " paraphernalia."

[3] I. *Entwurf,* §§ 1351, 1411 *seq.*, 1432.

[4] Germany, B. G., § 1439.

[5] *Ibid.*, §§ 1520 *seq.*, 1550 *seq.*

[6] Under individual systems, the proceeds of dotal property go to the husband alone.

[7] France, C. C., 1428; Germany, B. G., § 1439; Prussia, A. L. R., ii, 1, § 370.

[8] France, C. C., 1536; Germany, B. G., § 1441; Saxony, B. G., § 1693; Switz., *Vorentwurf,* § 215; *cf.* Prussia, A. L. R., ii, 1, § 221.

riage as a union of all of the material and spiritual interests of the parties. By virtue of the establishment of this system, all of the property which the parties possess is united into a common mass, to which is also added all of the property which either of the parties later acquires.[1] The joint title is substituted for the individual title without the necessity of a formal transfer.

The general rule has been subjected to numerous exceptions and modifications, and the perfect form of general community is not defined to-day in any important legislation. The legislations generally recognize that property may be excluded from the community by operation of law, by act of a third party or as a result of agreement between the parties.

The property of either party, which, by reason of entail or any limited title, cannot be alienated, is under statutory provision excluded from the common ownership. It falls under the class of dotal property and is administered for the benefit of the community.[2] Another example of property excluded from the community by operation of law, is wearing apparel and property intended for the exclusive personal use of one of the parties.[3] Most of the codes, however, do not establish this exception for systems of community. It is significant that the draft code of Switzerland provides that certain things shall become separate property, by operation of law, under all forms of matrimonial property relations. They include objects for exclusive personal use, the savings

[1] France, C. C., 1526; Germany, B. G., § 1438; Prussia, A. L. R., ii, 1, §§ 363, 371, 372; Saxony, B. G., § 1695; Switz., *Vorentwurf*, 244; Basle, Stat. Mch. 10, 1884, art. 2. In Austria the presumption is against the inclusion of future and inherited property, except it is expressly stipulated for each. B. G., § 1177.

[2] Germany, B. G., §§ 1439, 1525; Prussia, A. L. R., ii, 1, §§ 363, 370.

[3] For the wife: Prussia, A. L. R., ii, 1, § 364. For either party: Basle, Stat. Mch. 10, 1884, art. 3; Switz., *Vorentwurf*, 217.

of the wife, goods used by the latter in an independent industry or profession, and that which she acquires by her labor.[4] In Norway, also, where the general community has been greatly modified under the influence of modern conditions, it is the rule that a life insurance policy or annuity for the benefit of one of the parties, is his separate property unless express provisions exist to the contrary.[5]

Property is excluded from the joint ownership when it is acquired by gratuitous title, as a donation or succession, and the donor or testator has provided that it shall not become common.[6] The codes are not in harmony respecting the character of such property. According to the older codes, which emphasize the community of acquisitions, the property becomes dotal and the profits and income of the same accrue to the common mass as in the case of property excluded from community by operation of law.[7] On the other hand, the more recent legislations regard such property as separate in character.[8]

The principle of community may be profoundly modified as a result of agreement between the parties. They may exclude property from the common ownership and establish it as dotal or separate in character. Where there is a simple declaration that certain objects shall be excluded from the common mass, it would appear that the dotal features will be impressed upon such property If, however, the parties

[4] Switz., *Vorentwurf*, 217.

[5] Stat. June 29, 1888, art. 20; *cf.* France, Stat. July 20, 1886, *post*, § 18, note 10; Basle, Stat. Mch. 10, 1884, art. 21.

[6] France, C. C., 1401; Germany, B. G., §§ 1440, 1369; Prussia, A. L. R., ii, 1, §373; Saxony, B. G., § 1693; Switz., *Vorentwurf*, 216; Norway, Stat. June 29, 1889, arts. 20, 5; *cf.* Austria, B. G., § 1177.

[7] France, C. C., 1401, 1428; Prussia, A. L. R., ii, 1, §§ 371, 373, 405; Saxony, B. G., §§ 1693, 1695.

[8] Germany, B. G., §§ 1440, 1441, 1369; Switz., *Vorentwurf*, 215, 216; Norway, Stat. June 29, 1888, art. 20.

clearly indicate an intention that the administration and enjoyment, as well as the title, shall be reserved from the matrimonial property, the goods become separate in character.[9]

By these means the composition of the community may be so materially modified as to be practically identical with that of one of the types of limited community or even of an individual system. The general regulations governing general community would nevertheless continue to apply as respects obligations, etc., so far as they had not been modified by agreement between the parties.

§ 17. *Composition of Limited Community.*

(a) *Community of Movables and Acquisitions.*

The community of movables and acquisitions is the statutory system of the Civil Code of France, and has received acceptance in other states as a statutory or contractual system.[1] The general principles at the basis of this system are much the same as those which obtain in connection with general community.[2] Its fundamental point of departure from the latter is to be found in the modification of the composition of the community. Not only those objects which fall under the class of dotal or separate property in general community,[3] but also the immovables which either party possesses when the community arises, or subsequently

---

[9] Germany, B. G., § 1440; Prussia, A. L. R., ii, 1, § 360; Saxony, B. G., § 1693; Austria, B. G., § 1233; Norway, Stat. June 29, 1888, arts. 1, 8; France, C. C., 1536. The French Civil Code makes a clear distinction between mere exclusion of community and the establishment of separate property. *Ibid.*, 1529-1539; Viollet, *Précis*, p. 677 *seq.*

[1] See *ante*, § 13.

[2] The German code provides that this system shall be governed by the rules regulating general community so far as it is not otherwise expressly provided. B. G., § 1549.

[3] *Ante*, § 16.

acquires by title of donation or succession, are excluded from the common mass and do not constitute a part of the community property.[4] This exclusion results by operation of law and, in accordance with the general principle, such immovables become dotal and not separate property. The income and profits of such property, as acquisitions, not proceeding from donation or succession, accrue to the community.[5]

(b) *Community of Acquisitions.*

Under the system of community of acquisitions the common ownership is confined to such property as shall be acquired by either of the married parties during the existence of the community.[6] Acquisitions generally include the profits and proceeds of property owned by either party at the time the community commences. Such property is considered dotal though it may be reserved for separate use by agreement between the parties.

On the other hand, acquisitions do not embrace all property accruing to the parties during the existence of the

[4] France, C. C., 1402; Germany, B. G., § 1551; Switz., *Vorentwurf*, 264; Finland, the exclusion applies only to agricultural lands. In other respects this system agrees with general community, Stat. Apl. 15, 1889, c. i, arts. 2, 3.

[5] France, C. C., 1401; Germany, B. G., §§ 1550, 1551; Finland, Stat. Apl. 15, 1889, c. i, art. 6; *contra*, Switz., *Vorentwurf*, 264, which makes such property separate in character. The parties may stipulate, however, that such property shall be subject to marital administration and usufruct, in which case the acquisitions accrue to the husband, and, under the rules of community, will become common. *Ibid.*, 265.

[6] France, C. C., 1498; Spain, C. C., 1392; Italy, C. C., 1436; Germany, B. G., § 1519; Prussia, A. L. R., ii, 1, § 396; Switz., *Vorentwurf*, 266; Ariz., R. S., 1887, §§ 2100, 2102; Cal., C. C., §§ 162, 164; Idaho, R. S., 1887, §§ 2495, 2497; La., C. C., 1402; Nev., G. S., 1885, §§ 499, 500; Texas, R. S., 1895, arts. 2967, 2968; Wash., G. S., 1891, §§ 1397, 1399; in New Mexico, the community appears to be primarily intended as a provision for the survivor and to begin only at the dissolution of the marriage. Before that time it is a simple account be-. tween the parties, each remaining owner of his acquisitions. C. L., 1897, § 2030

community. That property which, under general community, is excluded from common ownership by operation of law, will likewise retain its individual character under the community of acquisitions and will be considered dotal property.[7] The same rule generally obtains respecting property falling to either party by donation of succession so far as the donor or testator has not indicated a desire that it shall become common[8] or separate[9] in character.

Some of the American states that have established a community of acquisitions have limited it to the products of the personal industry of both parties. All property owned by either party at the time of the marriage, or acquired afterwards by donation or succession is declared to be the separate property of such party, and the increase and proceeds of the same have a like character.[10]

Dotal property will also include all objects acquired as compensation for damages to or by way of exchange for property which has the dotal character.[11]

Separate property is determined by the same general principles as were indicated in connection with general community,[12] but particular exceptions arise. Thus, the code of Germany excludes separate property of the husband under both forms of limited community.[13] The individual title of

[7] Germany, B. G., § 1522; Spain, C. C., 1403, 1404; *cf. ante*, § 16.

[8] France, C. C., 1498, 1401, 1402; Italy, C. C., 1435 : Spain, C. C., 1396; Germany, B. G., §1521; Prussia, A. L. R., ii, 1, §§ 402, 405; Switz., *Vorentwurf*, 266, 226; Idaho, R. S., 1887, §§ 2495, 2497; La., C. C., 2402; Texas, if real property it becomes separate in character, but the husband has the administration of the same. R. S., 1895, art. 2967; *cf. post*, § 42, note 1.

[9] Germany, B. G., §§ 1526, 1369; Switz., *Vorentwurf*, 215, 216.

[10] Ariz., R. S., 1887, § 2100; Cal., C. C., §§ 162, 163; Nev., G. S., 1885, § 499; Wash., G. S., 1891, §§ 1397, 1398.

[11] France, C. C., 1407, 1408; Spain, C. C., 1396, 1402; Germany, B. G., §1524; Switz., *Vorentwurf*, 206.

[12] *Ante*, § 16.   [14] B. G., §§ 1526, 1555.

each party is preserved in a part of his property which regularly becomes dotal by operation of the statute, whereas under general community the entire property, as a rule, becomes common. As the husband has the administration of the dotal property, a special separate estate was not considered necessary in his case. It also appears that in Italy, separate property cannot be established for either party by contract or otherwise. If the parties elect to live under the community system, all of their acquisitions, which do not become communal, will be treated as dotal property.[14]

Under the community of acquisitions uncertainty will frequently arise as to whether the title to certain property is common or individual. In order to protect the interests of innocent third parties and to simplify the property relations between the married parties, a presumption is raised, analogous to that which obtains in favor of creditors, respecting the ownership of movables found in the possession of the married parties.[15] It will be presumed that the existing property belongs to both parties jointly. This presumption may be rebutted by the production of public titles, inventories, *etc.*[16]

§ 18. *Products of the Personal Industry of the Wife.*

Determined efforts have been made in many states still further to restrict the community by excluding therefrom the products of the personal industry of the wife so far as such activity does not pertain to the household or the business of the husband. The movement has received the support of those who advocate the emancipation of the married woman from the disabilities imposed upon her by the

[14] C. C., 1434–1436.

[15] *Ante*, § 5, notes 15, 16.

[16] France, C. C., 1499: Italy, C. C., 1437; Germany, B. G., §§ 1527, 1528; Prussia, A. L. R., ii, 1, §§ 397, 401.

law. They insist that such property shall become the separate property of the married woman, and that she shall be permitted to exercise such powers over the same as the married man exercises over the products of his industry.

On the other hand, many who oppose the principle of separation of property interests of married parties, have supported the demand for a reform in the law governing acquisitions which proceed from the personal labor of the wife. One of the greatest hardships connected with the system of community, as well as with the English common law, is the fact that property which is the result of the arduous labor of the woman, and probably the sole dependence of the family, may be taken and dissipated by an idle, drunken and vicious husband. The only recourse of the wife is a judicial proceeding for separation of property or divorce. If she has a natural hesitancy to expose her domestic affairs by taking public legal proceedings, or, as is often the case where the evil is greatest, if the expense of the process proves an obstacle, her economic interests are wholly at the mercy of the husband. Even where the extreme cases do not exist, economic principles justify the reform. The energy and economy of the woman will be increased to the extent that she is accorded a control over the results of her activity.

The systems of individual property have generally accorded the married woman adequate protection in this respect.[1] Among the community systems the movement has been successful to a certain extent in the Scandinavian countries, Geneva and the American states, but in the French and Spanish civil codes, as well as in the legislations which recognize community as a contractual system, the old principles have not, as yet, been modified.[2]

[1] *Post*, §§ 26, 32, 39.

[2] France, C. C., 1401, 1498; Italy, C. C., 1436; Spain, C. C., 1401; Germany,

The proposition to secure the reform by making the products of the industry of the wife her separate property, encountered severe opposition on the ground that such a system would not correspond to the social customs and conceptions which are at the basis of the marriage and the family.[3] Moreover, it was argued that it would be inequitable to permit the wife to retain exclusive ownership of the proceeds of her industry while all of the husband's acquisitions were brought into the common mass in which the wife takes an equal share. The interests of creditors have also been advanced as an objection to the proposed plan.

As a result of these considerations the Scandinavian countries do not exclude the wife's earnings from the joint ownership, but give her an exclusive right of disposing of the same,[4] and exempt such property, during the life of the wife, from execution for the husband's debts unless they have been contracted with her consent.[5] If the industry of the wife is carried on for the most part with the capital of the husband, these provisions will not apply.[6]

B. G., § 1524; Prussia, A. L. R., ii, 1, §§ 363, 396; Saxony, B. G., § 1695; Austria, B. G., § 1177.

[3] Pascaud, " Le Droit de Femme mariée aux Produits de son Travail," *Rev. Pol. et Parle.*, vol. ix, p. 571 *seq.*; Guntzberger, p. 225 *seq.*

[4] Denmark, Stat. May 7, 1880, art. 1, *An. étran.*, vol. 10, p. 533; Norway, Stat. June 29, 1888, art. 31; Finland, Stat. Apl. 15, 1889, c. ii, art. 3. In Sweden a statute of Dec. 11, 1874, amending the law governing matrimonial relations, provides that a married woman may stipulate in the marriage contract that she shall have the free administration of her individual property and of the things that she acquires by her labor, F = S., 1874, no. 109, pp. 1–3; *cf. An. étran.*, vol. 4, pp. 566, 567.

[5] *Contra* in Finland, where such property may be taken after the other common property and the individual property of the husband has been exhausted.   Stat. Apl. 15, 1889, c. iv, art. 2.

[6] Norway, Stat. June 29, 1888, art. 31; in Denmark the same is true if the capital belongs to the community.   Stat. May 7, 1880, art. 1, *An. étran.*, vol. 10, p. 533.

A recent statute of Geneva takes a more advanced position. It accords the wife under all systems the same right over the proceeds of her personal industry as is possessed by the married woman under the system of separate property.[7] A qualification has been made, however, under the influence of the considerations indicated above. All of such property must be added to the common mass at the dissolution of the community, unless the wife or her heirs renounce her share in the joint property.[8] She will not be permitted to share in the results of her husband's activity unless she is willing to contribute her earnings to the common partnership.

Attempts are being made to bring about similar reforms in other European states. The Belgian Chamber, in 1899, considered a measure granting married women the right to make small deposits in savings banks and to dispose of the same for household necessities.[9] Such deposits were to be exempt from execution by the creditors of the husband. Similar statutes have been enacted in France, but so far as the system of community obtains between the parties, the sums deposited continue to be held in common and the wife has simply a right of limited administration over the same.[10]

In France, also, the movement to accord the married woman similar rights over her earnings, independent of their deposit in a bank, has achieved some success, and it appears

[7] Stat. Nov. 7, 1894, art. 1, *An. étran*, vol. 24, p. 634.

[8] *Ibid.*, art. 4.

[9] German newspapers of September 13, 1899.

[10] Stat. Apl. 9, 1881, art. 6, *Bull. des lois*, xii, Sér., vol. 22, p. 666; Stat. July 20, 1886, art. 13, *ibid.*, vol. 33, p. 279. The statute of July 20, 1886, provides for the purchase of an annuity by a certain number of deposits. If the deposits are made by a married party, the annuity will be held as individual property, but an equal amount will be purchased for each spouse. *Cf.* recent acts of Louisiana, *ante*, § 3, note 18.

that its purpose is on the point of being accomplished. Two distinct reforms are proposed. One is directed to the evil which exists where the husband's conduct jeopards the interests of the wife and the expense of the proceeding precludes the relief afforded by the judicial separation of property. It is proposed that where the husband by his misconduct injuriously affects the welfare of the household, his wife, without demanding separation of goods, may be authorized by a justice of the peace to collect the products of her labor and to freely dispose of the same. Moreover, if abandoned by her husband, she may demand a certain portion of his income. Under the other proposition married women, in general, are given the right of free disposition over the products of their personal industry, but such acquisitions continue to belong to the common mass, and, as such, are subject to the claims of the creditors of the husband.[11] These measures were considered by the Chamber of Deputies, and, in 1895, referred to a committee which harmonized and combined the same. Following the latter proposition, the wife, without any special authorization, is entitled to dispose of the products of her labor. Incorporated with this is the provision that a wife deserted by her husband may be authorized to collect a share of his income. Upon the favorable report of the committee the bill passed the Chamber of Deputies in 1896, but it has not as yet received the approval of the Senate.[12]

The American states which recognize a community of acquisitions, regard the earnings of the wife as common property, but generally give her a right of disposition over the same which is as extensive as that obtained under the

---

[11] *An. fran.*, vol. 14, p. 16, notes 5, 6; Guntzberger, pp. 205, 206, 218.

[12] *An. fran.*, vols. 15, p. 11, note 8, 16, p. 9, note 6; Pascaud, " Le Droit de la Femme mariée aux Produits de son Travail," *Rev. Pol. et Parle.*, vol. ix, p. 579.

Geneva statute.[13] Moreover, if the wife is living separate
from her husband, her earnings become her separate
property.[14]

Finally, it is worthy of note that the draft code of Switzerland proposes to go further than any of the existing legislations, except those recognizing separate property as the
statutory system, by providing that under all systems of
matrimonial property the acquisitions proceeding from the
labor of the wife shall be her separate property.[15]

§ 19. *Obligations of the Community.*

(a) *General Community.*

According to the ideal principle at the basis of the
system of general community, the obligations of each of
the parties, whether incurred before or during the existence
of the community, should become common. This theory,
however, fails of realization to an even greater degree than
is true with respect to the composition of the community.
Considerations of equity have led to a modification of the
general principle.

The legislations recognize in general, that the common
property is liable for the obligations of each of the married
parties.[1] This liability, however, does not extend to

---

[13] There is a general exemption of such property from liability for the husband's
debts.   Cal., C. C., § 168; Nev., G. S., 1885, § 511; N. M., C. L., 1897, § 1509;
Wash., G. S., 1891, § 1402; *cf.* recent acts of Louisiana, *ante*, § 3, note 18.

[14] Ariz., R. S., 1887, § 2101; Cal., C. C., § 169; Idaho, R. S., 1887, § 2502;
Nev., G. S., 1885, § 512; Wash., G. S., 1891, § 1403.

[15] Switz., *Vorentwurf*, 217.

[1] France, C. C., 1409; Austria, B. G., § 1235; Norway, Stat. June 29, 1888,
arts. 17, 23; Germany, B. G., § 1459; Saxony, B. G., § 1696; Prussia, A. L. R.,
ii, 1, §§ 391, 394, but if the ante-nuptial debts of one party exceed his contribution to the common fund, the other may move for separation of property within
two years after marriage, in which case only the individual property of the debtor
can be held for such debts. *Ibid.*, §§ 392, 393.

obligations arising from post-nuptial contracts entered into by the wife without the authorization of her husband, except where she has an independent right of administration over the common property.[2] The same is true of obligations arising in connection with property which is excluded from the joint ownership and subjected to the administration of the wife.[3] Aside from these exceptions, the obligations of each of the parties, whether arising out of contract or tort, and including the expenses of judicial proceedings, bind the community.[4] This is true, however, only as regards third parties.

There is another departure from the principle of ideal community in the recognition of certain obligations, which, as between the parties themselves, do not bind the common property, but fall to the charge of the individual debtor. These, include obligations arising from the criminal acts of either party,[5] and those incurred in connection with the administration of the separate property of either party.[6]

It must also be noted that even as regards third parties, the obligations that bind the common property are not true communal obligations. As such, they would bind not only

[2] France, C. C., 1409, 1419; Germany, B. G., § 1460; Prussia, A. L, R., ii, 1, § 389; Norway, Stat. June 29, 1888, art. 17; Switz., *Vorentwurf*, 249, 250.

[3] Germany, B. G., §§ 1461, 1462; Prussia, A. L. R., ii, 1, § 389; Norway, Stat. June 29, 1888, art. 17.

[4] In France the common property is not liable for fines imposed as a result of criminal acts of the wife, C. C., 1424.

[5] France, C. C., 1424; Germany, B. G., § 1463; Prussia, A. L. R., ii, 1, §§ 385, 390; Norway, extends to any obligation resulting from the wrongful act of either party, Stat. June 29, 1888, arts. 17, 18.

[6] France, C. C., 1409, 1412, 1437; Germany, B. G., § 1463; Prussia, A. L. R., ii, 1, §§ 385, 390; Norway, Stat. June 29, 1888, arts. 17, 18. For other particular provisions respecting compensation due from one party to the other for obligations satisfied out of the common property, see France, C. C., §§ 1438, 1439; Germany, B. G., §§ 1464–1467; Norway, Stat. June 29, 1888, art. 23; Switz., *Vorentwurf*, 252.

the common property but each party individually. The legislations agree, however, in exempting the wife from any personal liability for such obligations, except where they fall to her charge as between the parties themselves.[7] On the other hand, this privilege is not extended to the husband, who is generally personally responsible for all obligations that bind the common property.[8]

The explanation of these departures from the strict principle of community is to be found partially in the exceptions arising respecting the composition of general community,[9] but chiefly in the extensive exclusive rights of administration which are enjoyed by the husband.[10] This power might seriously endanger the interests of the wife if she were to be held liable for the obligations which bind the common property.

(b) *Community of Movables and Acquisitions.*

The obligations of the common association under the system of community of movables and acquisitions are determined by the same general rules as regulate the obligations of the general community.[11] As between the parties, also, the same principles are at the basis of the compensation and contribution due for the individual debts which are discharged out of the common funds.[12]

---

[7] *Denkschrift,* p. 295; see, also, *post,* § 24.

[8] France, only for a moiety of those which are personal to his wife, C. C., 1485; Germany, for obligations personal to his wife such liability expires at the dissolution of the community, B. G., § 1459; Switz., *Vorentwurf,* 251.

[9] *Ante,* § 16.

[10] *Post,* § 20.

[11] Germany, B. G., § 1549; Finland, Stat. Apl. 15, 1889, c. iv, arts. 2, 4; see notes, *ante,* (a).

[12] But in Finland, ante-nuptial obligations are separate as between the parties, and the Norwegian statute is followed in applying the same rule to obligations arising from wrongful acts, Stat. Apl. 15, 1889, c. iv, arts. 1, 5; *cf.* Norway, Stat. June 29, 1888, arts. 23, 17, 18.

Finland has departed from the general rule respecting personal liability for the debts which are binding upon the common property. It exempts the husband as well as the wife from liability for those debts of the other party, which, as between the parties, do not fall to the charge of the community.[13] Where the parties have obliged themselves equally, or where the wife, with the authorization of the husband, has contracted obligations in the interest of the household, both parties are bound; and if the individual property of one fails to liquidate his share, the deficiency will be satisfied out of the property of the other.[14] In other respects the general rule is followed.[15]

(c) Community of Acquisitions.

The system of community of acquisitions does not contemplate any general blending of the property interests of the married parties. The community does not embrace the capital stock of either party, and hence the principle that all obligations of the parties should bind the common property does not obtain. The common property is constituted for the primary purpose of sustaining the matrimonial charges, and is liable for the same whether they are incurred by the husband or by the wife, if within the sphere of her administration. As all of the profits of dotal property fall into the common mass, the latter must sustain the necessary charges binding upon such property or connected with its administration or preservation.[16]

With respect to other obligations, the principle would seem to require that they shall have been created for the benefit of the common property or connected with its ad-

---

[13] Stat. Apl. 15, 1889, c. iv, arts. 1, 5, 6.

[14] *Ibid.*, art. 2.   [15] *Ibid.*, art. 3.

[16] France, C. C., 1498, 1409; Spain, C. C., 1408; Italy, C. C., 1434, 1435; Germany, B. G., § 1531; Prussia, A. L, R., ii, 1, §§ 407, 408; Saxony, B. G., § 1696; Switz., *Vorentwurf*, 266, 248, 250; Texas, R. S., 1895, arts. 1201, 2970.

ministration, in order to be binding upon the community. The states are not in accord upon this question. The French Civil Code and the legislations that have felt its influence, recognize the logical development of the principle and exclude the ante-nuptial obligations of each of the parties.[17] A practical difficulty in the way of the realization of this principle is the fact that the husband is the general administrator of the common property and can freely dispose of the same. He is thereby enabled to use the common fund in the liquidation of his ante-nuptial obligations. It is probable that most of the legislations would recognize the right of the husband's ante-nuptial creditors to seize the common property, at least after all of the common creditors had been satisfied, but would require the husband to make compensation at the dissolution of the community. This is particularly true among the German states, where the tendency is to regard the husband, who is the head of the community, as occupying much the same position as under the system of marital administration and usufruct. Accordingly, the new German code makes the acquisitions which constitute the common property, responsible for the ante-nuptial debts of the husband, while excluding liability for such obligations of the wife.[18]

So far as concerns post-nuptial obligations, the rule obtains as under other systems of community that the common

[17] France, C. C., 1498; Italy, C. C., 1435; Spain, if all communal obligations have been satisfied, the common property may be held for the ante-nuptial debts of either party, if the debtor has not sufficient individual property, C. C., 1410; La., C. C., 2403; cf. Austria, B. G., § 1235; Texas, R. S., 1895, arts. 2973, 2219; Wash., G. S. 1891, § 1413.

[18] B. G., § 1530; in Prussia (A. L. R., ii, 1, §§ 407, 408), and the Swiss draft code (Vorentwurf, 266, 248), the rule is the same as under general community that the ante-nuptial obligations of each party bind the community. Cf. Ariz., R. S., 1887, § 2105; Cal., C. C., § 170; Idaho, R. S., 1887, § 2503; Nev., G. S., 1885, § 514.

property is liable for the debts and obligations contracted by the husband during the existence of the community.[19] The case is different, however, as regards post-nuptial obligations incurred by the wife. The community of acquisitions is not regularly liable for such obligations. It is only in those cases where the wife has undertaken the same with the express or implied authorization of her husband or has an independent right of communal administration that her acts will be binding upon the common property.[20] Accordingly, obligations arising from her torts or unlawful acts do not bind the common fund.[21]

Claims for compensation by one party against the other on account of personal obligations which have been discharged out of the common property, are determined in the same manner as under other systems of community. Inasmuch, however, as the ante-nuptial obligations of the wife are not supported by the joint property, the husband is required to make compensation where his obligations, arising before the beginning of the community, have been liquidated out of the common fund.[22]

The personal liability for the common obligations is likewise regulated by the same rules as obtain for general community.[23] The exemptions of the wife and the extensive

[19] France, C. C., 1498, 1409; Italy, C. C., 1434, 1438; Spain, C. C., 1408; Germany, B. G., § 1530; Prussia, A. L. R., ii, i, § 407; Switz., *Vorentwurf*, 249.

[20] France, C. C., 1498; Spain, C. C., 1408; Italy, C. C., 1436; Germany, B. G., §§ 1532–1534; Prussia, A. L. R., ii, 1, § 408; Switz., *Vorentwurf*, 250; Ariz., R. S., 1887, § 2107; Cal., C. C., § 167; Idaho, R. S., 1887, § 5860; La., C. C., 2403, 1786; Nev., G. S., 1885, § 538; Texas, R. S., 1895, arts, 2973, 2219, 2970, 2971.

[21] In Spain, this is true of both parties, but if the common debts have been satisfied, the payment of such obligations may be demanded out of the common property if the debtor has insufficient individual property, C. C., 1410.

[22] Germany, B. G., § 1536; Spain, C. C., 1410.

[23] *Ante* (a). In Prussia, however, the husband as well as the wife does not ncur any liability for the individual debts of the other, A. L. R., ii. 1, § 406; *cf.*

liabilities of the husband correspond to their respective fields of administration, and will be better appreciated after the consideration of such functions.

§ 20. *Administration of the Common Property.*

In order to carry out the ideal principle of community, the administration of the property should be entrusted to the married parties jointly. The management and disposition should represent the united action of the two parties. While this principle of the " gesammte Hand " has not failed to find advocates,[1] the legislations have modified it in the same degree as they have abandoned other embodiments of the broad communal idea. Thus, it is generally recognized that the husband has the administration of the common property and exercises the right in his own name.[2] This power of administration does not, however, confer an unqualified power of disposition over the common goods. Considerations of the interests of the wife have led to limitations upon certain acts. The principle of common administration is also retained in provisions that the co-operation of the wife

Ariz., R. S. 1887, § 2105; Cal., C. C., §§ 170, 171; Idaho, R. S., 1887, §§ 2503, 2504; Nev., G. S., 1885, §§ 514, 515; Wash., G. S., 1891, § 1413.

[1] Professor Gierke, in his criticism of the first draft of the German Code, argues that if any single statutory system is to be created it should be general community, and insists upon its establishment in accordance with the ideal principle of community (Gierke, *Entwurf*, pp. 417, 425 *seq.*); *cf.* Proelsz und Raschke, *Die Frau im neuen bürgerlichen Gesetzbuch*, p. 14. In the first drafts of the Code Napoléon the system of common administration was introduced, but this was later abandoned for the exclusive administration of the husband, Guntzberger, pp. 39, 40; *cf.* provisions of Swiss draft code, *post*, note 6.

[2] France, C. C., 1421; Italy, C. C., 1438; Spain, C. C., 1412; Germany, B. G., §§ 1443, 1519, 1549; Prussia, A. L. R., ii, 1, § 377, 411; Saxony, B. G., § 1697; Norway, Stat. June 29, 1888, art. 14; Finland, Stat. Apl. 15, 1889, c. ii, art. 1; Basle, Stat. Mch. 10, 1884, art. 2; Switz., *Vorentwurf*, 245, 266; Ariz., R. S., 1887, § 2102; Cal., C. C., § 172; Idaho, R. S., 1887, § 2505; La., C. C., 2404; Nev., G. S., 1885, § 504; Texas, R. S., 1895, Art. 2968; Wash., G. S., §§ 1399, 1400.

shall be necessary to the validity of particular dispositions. Finally, an independent sphere of administration of the common property is given the married woman.

The limitations upon the power of the husband rest upon considerations of the nature of the act or the character of the property to be affected thereby. His donations out of the common property, except where made in fulfilment of a customary duty, are dependent upon the consent of the wife or are forbidden in general terms.³ Under some legislations, acts whereby the husband undertakes to dispose of the whole or a general part of the common property, are likewise conditioned.⁴ The attitude of legislations towards real property has generally led to similar requirements for the consent of the wife, or the joint action of the parties where common immovables are to be encumbered or alienated.⁵

³ Italy, C. C., 1438; Spain, C. C., 1413–1415; Germany, B. G., § 1446; Norway, where they exceed one-tenth in value of the common goods, Stat. June 29, 1888, art. 14; Switz., *Vorentwurf*, 246; in Prussia the husband has the general right to make donations, but the wife may contest the same where she would have such right if donation proceeded from her, and is entitled to compensation at the end of the community, A. L. R., ii, 1, §§ 380–383; in France (C. C., 1422), and Louisiana (C. C., 2404), the prohibition does not extend to particular donations of movables except the husband has retained the usufruct of the same. While most of the American States have not limited the husband's power in this matter, except as regards testamentary dispositions, a California statute of March 31, 1891, makes all donations of common property dependent upon written consent of wife, Stat. and Amend., 1891, p. 425.

⁴ Germany, B. G., § 1444; Prussia, A. L. R., ii, 1, §§ 378, 379; Saxony, B. G., § 1698; Switz., *Vorentwurf*, 246. The legislations that have followed the Code Napoléon do not distinguish between acts of general and of particular disposition except as regards gifts (see preceding note), and in some cases dispositions affecting immovables. It is necessary to note that the general community does not obtain as the statutory system in these legislations, and is absolutely prohibited in some (*ante*, § 13, note 18).

⁵ Germany, B. G., § 1445; Prussia, A. L. R., ii, 1, §§ 378, 379; Saxony, B. G., § 1698; Norway, if brought by wife into community, Stat. June 29, 1888, art. 14; Finland, Stat. Apl. 15, 1889, c. ii, art. 2; Basle, Stat. Mch. 10, 1884, art. 4; Wash.,

The draft code of Switzerland preserves the principle of joint action to a greater degree than the existing legislations. It provides that all dispositions of either party, affecting the common property, which exceed acts of ordinary administration, are subject to the consent or joinder of the other. Such consent, however, will be presumed except where the third party has knowledge to the contrary, or where it is clear that the property belongs to both parties jointly.[6]

In order to avoid the damage to the common economic interests which may result from disagreement between the parties, it is generally provided that if the wife refuses her consent, or for other reasons it cannot be obtained, the court may supply the same if the conditions of the administration justify the act.[7]

The married woman is generally given a limited right of administration of the common property. This is for the most part restricted[8] to acts performed within the circle of her domestic activity,[9] or in an independent business which she carries on with the consent of her husband.[10] It has been increased to the extent that she has been given a con-

---

G. S., 1891, § 1400. The other legislations do not limit the husband's power in this respect (*cf.* preceding note), but, in American states, if the common real estate is occupied as a homestead, acts of disposition of the same will be subject to the joinder of the wife. See *post*, § 41.

[6] Switz., *Vorentwurf*, 346; *cf.* Prussia, A. L. R., ii, 1, § 387.

[7] Germany, B. G., § 1447; Prussia, A. L. R., ii, 1, §§ 387, 388; Basle, Stat. Mch. 10, 1884, art. 4; Switz., *Vorentwurf*, 247, 199; *cf*, Finland, Stat. Apl. 15, 1889, c. ii, art. 2.

[8] But in Norway any obligation contracted by the wife for the benefit of the community binds the common property, Stat. June 29, 1888, art. 17.

[9] *Ante*, § 8.

[10] *Ante*, § 6; France, C. C., 220; Italy, C. C., 135; Germany, B. G., §§ 1452, 1405; Prussia, A. L. R., ii, 1, §§ 389, 335-337; Basle, Stat. Mch. 10, 1884, art. 8; La., C. C., 131.

trol over the products of her personal industry.[11] With respect to other acts affecting the common property, the wife must, in general, obtain the authorization of her husband.[12] Where the circumstances do not justify a refusal of authorization by the husband, his consent may be supplied by the court.[13] The French code, while recognizing the right of the court to supply the consent of the husband so as to validate an act of the wife,[14] does not permit her to bind the common property by such act. Unless the husband consents to the same it will bind only the individual property of the wife.[15]

The position of the wife, as a partner in the community, is recognized by granting her the right of temporary administration, in case of the absence or disability of the husband, where damage might result if the matter were delayed.[16] In systems following the Code Napoléon, however, the wife, even in such cases, must receive the authorization of the court in order to bind the common property.[17]

It is the general rule that if the husband is under guardianship, he will be represented by his guardian in the administration of the common property.[18] The tendency,

[11] *Ante*, § 18; in the Swiss draft code, such products, as well as the goods employed in her trade or industry, are the separate property of the wife and are hence entirely excluded from common administration, *Vorentwurf*, 217.

[12] The German code gives the wife the sole right of accepting or rejecting donations, successions, *etc.*, B. G., § 1453; *cf.* also, *ibid.*, §§ 1449, 1454. *Cf.* acts in France and Louisiana giving wife right of administration over her deposits in savings banks, *ante*, § 3, notes 7, 18.

[13] Germany, B. G., § 1451; Saxony, B. G., § 1644; *Cf.* Switz., *Vorentwurf*, 247; *ante*, § 3.

[14] C. C., 218, 219.   [15] *Ibid.*, 1426; *cf.* Spain, C. C., 1416.

[16] Germany, B. G., § 1450; Prussia, A. L. R., ii, 1, §§ 202–204, 327, 389; Saxony, B. G., § 1643; *cf.* Norway, Stat. June 29, 1888, art. 17.

[17] France, C. C., 124, 1427, C. C. P., 863; Spain, C. C., 188; La., C. C., 132.

[18] Germany, B. G., § 1457; *Motive*, vol. iv, p. 364; but see *contra*, Saxony, B. G., § 1700; Spain, C. C., 225, where the right of administration is accorded the wife.

however, is to give the wife the right and privilege of being appointed guardian of her husband.[19]

Practical considerations have led to the substitution of the individual for the common principle in the administration of the joint property. The husband is the head of the family and, as such, is the natural administrator of its economic interests. The property of the wife is safeguarded by requiring her consent to certain acts, by constituting securities in her favor,[20] and by enabling her to take measures for withdrawing the administration from the husband whenever his acts imperil her interests.[21] The fact, moreover, that the wife incurs no personal responsibility for such acts of administration is at once a cause and a result of the extensive powers accorded to the husband.[22]

§ 21. *Administration of the Dotal and Separate Property.*

The dotal property of the married parties is administered by the husband for their joint benefit and profit. The rules determining the scope and extent of his powers are for the most part the same as those which regulate the administration of dotal property under the system of marital administration and usufruct, and will be considered in connection with the discussion of that system.[1]

Separate property, under communal systems, is governed by the general regulations obtaining for the system of separate property.[2]

[19] *Motive,* vol. iv, p. 364; Spain, C. C., 220, 230; La., Acts, 1894, No. 45; *contra,* France, C. C., 442.

[20] *Post,* § 22.   [21] *Post,* § 23, (b).

[22] *Ante,* § 19, (a), note, 7.

[1] *Post,* § 27. The code of Germany and the draft code of Switzerland provide that dotal property, under communal systems, shall be administered according to the rules regulating the system of marital administration and usufruct. Germany, B. G., §§ 1439, 1525, 1550; Switz., *Vorentwurf,* 266.

[2] *Ante,* § 15; Germany, B. G., §§ 1444, 1526, 1549; Switz., *Vorentwurf,* 264, 215.

§ 22. *Protection of the Wife's Property.*

Under the general community, the property of the wife is united with that of the husband to form a common mass. If joint administration exists, no particular provisions are necessary for the protection of the wife's interests. But where the husband is recognized as having an individual right of administration, the rights of the wife may be seriously endangered. Most of the legislations recognize this fact, and in according the husband extensive powers of disposition, they have generally furnished the wife with certain means for the protection of her property. Particular qualifications upon the husband's power of disposing of the common property have been indicated,[1] and it has also been shown that the wife is entirely relieved from any personal liability for the administration of her husband.[2]

The efficiency of the common administration would be seriously impaired if the wife could hold the husband accountable for the character of his administration. The communal idea is therefore retained in this respect. It is sometimes recognized, however, that if the husband damages the common property with the design of injuring the interests of the wife, he may be compelled to make compensation.[3]

The wife has not, in general, any right to a particular security on account of her share in the common property.[4]

---

[1] *Ante,* § 20.   [2] *Ante,* § 19.

[3] Germany, B. G., § 1456; *cf.* Prussia, A. L. R., ii, 1, §383; Norway, Stat. June 29, 1888, art. 16.

[4] In Basle City, the wife in case her husband becomes bankrupt, has a claim against the mass for the whole of the fortune she has contributed to the common property, and is carried as a privileged creditor for the moiety of such amount. Stat. Mch. 10, 1884, art. 11. Prior to this statute she had a privilege for the whole amount. *An. étran.,* vol. 14, p. 545. The federal law of bankruptcy provides that the privileged share cannot exceed one-half. Alexander, *Konk. G.,* p. 307. The draft Swiss code gives the wife the right to demand security for the prop-

It appears reasonable that, in so far as she possesses dotal property, it should be protected in the same degree as under other systems of matrimonial property.[5] This is the position taken by the new German code.[6] The title of dotal and separate property may be protected against the presumption that existing goods belong to the husband, or are common in character,[7] by means of a properly authenticated inventory.[8]

The code of Saxony[9] gave the wife efficient protection in her right to demand that the administration of the common property be given to her whenever her rights are endangered through the bad administration of her husband, and the same is true in Spain[10] when the husband is declared a spendthrift. In most of the legislations, however, the married woman is limited for the protection of her interests in the common property to her right to move for a dissolution of the community.[11]

§ 23. *Dissolution of the Community.*[1]

(a) *As the Legal Result of Bankruptcy.*

Some of the legislations recognize that the community is

erty she contributes, but such claim will justify the husband in demanding a dissolution of the community. *Vorentwurf,* 213, 199.

[5] *Post,* §§ 29, 30, 34.

[6] B. G., §§ 1439, 1525, 1550, 1391.

[7] *Ante,* § 5.

[8] France, C. C., 1499, 1504, 1510; Italy, C. C., 1437; Spain, C. C., 1407; Germany, B. G., § 1528; Prussia, A. L. R., ii, 1, §§ 374-376, 397-401; Norway, Stat. June 29, 1888, art. 6; Finland, Stat. Mch. 10, 1889, c. iii, art. 4; Ariz., R. S., 1887, §§ 2611-2616; Cal., C. C., §§ 165-166; Idaho, R. S., 1887, §§ 2500, 2501; La., C. C., 2405; Nev., G. S., 1885, §§ 501-503; Texas, R. S., 1895, arts. 4654-4659.

[9] B. G., § 1700.   [10] C. C., 225.   [11] *Post,* §23, (b).

[1] The American legislations, with the exception of Louisiana, do not recognize a dissolution of the community except as a result of a dissolution of the marriage, but a partial separation of property results whenever the wife is living separate from her husband. See *ante,* § 18, note 14.

dissolved by operation of law, as a result of the opening of bankruptcy proceedings over the property of either party.[2] This rule has been accepted, for the most part, only in those states where the bulk of the wife's property is dotal. In general community or community of movables and acquisitions the common property constitutes the major portion, and a rule by which the dissolution of the community followed as the necessary legal result of the bankruptcy of either party, would involve a serious breach in the nature of the matrimonial property relations.

(b) *Upon Demand of One of the Parties.*

While most of the legislations do not accept the principle that bankruptcy dissolves the community of property, there is general agreement in recognizing the right to move for a dissolution in cases of bankruptcy or insolvency, or whenever the irregular administration or excessive obligations of one party are such as to endanger the rights of the other in the common property.[3]

An important ground for demanding the dissolution of the community, which has been introduced in recent legislation, is the failure of the husband to fulfil his obligation to furnish support for his wife and children.[4]

[2] Austria, B. G., § 1262; Basle, Stat. Mch. 10, 1884, arts. 1, 12; Switzerland, if claims of the creditors are not satisfied, *Vorentwurf,* 197; Germany, limited to the bankruptcy of the husband, and obtains only under community of acquisitions. B. G., § 1543.

[3] Upon demand of either party: Germany, B. G., §§ 1468, 1469, 1542; Prussia, A. L. R., ii, 1, § 421; Finland, Stat. Apl. 15, 1889, c. v.; Switz., *Vorentwurf,* 197, 198; upon demand of the wife: France, C. C., 1443; Italy, C. C., 1442; Norway, Stat. June 29, 1888, art. 38; Basle, Stat. Mch. 10, 1884, art. 40; La., C. C., 2425; for rule in Saxony (B. G., § 1700), and Spain (C. C., 225), see *ante,* § 22.

[4] Germany, B. G., §§ 1468, 1542; Geneva, Stat. Nov. 7, 1894, art. 5 (*An. étran.,* vol. 24, p. 635), extending provisions of art. 1443 of the French Civil Code, which is deficient in this respect; Switz., *Vorentwurf,* 198; Norway, if husband has abandoned wife, Stat. June 29, 1888, art. 34; *cf. ante,* § 18, notes 11, 12, proposed statute in France according wife, in case of misconduct of her husband, a partial separation of property so far as regards her earnings.

Among the other grounds recognized as justifying a demand for the dissolution of common property relations are the placing of the husband under guardianship,[5] his disappearance[6] or his disposition of matters without the necessary consent of the wife.[7]

(c) *By Mutual Agreement.*

In general, all systems, except those that prohibit postnuptial marriage contracts, permit the community to be dissolved as a result of agreement between the parties. As regards innocent third parties, particular formalities must be observed, but as between the parties, the dissolution is effective from the conclusion of the agreement.[8]

(d) *By Divorce or Judicial Separation of the Parties.*

The dissolution of the marriage by decree of divorce or nullity regularly produces a separation of the property interests of the parties.[9] The same effect generally results from a judicial separation of the parties which does not involve a dissolution of the matrimonial relation.[10] Under some of the systems, however, such separation does not

---

[5] Germany, in case of community of acquisitions, B. G., §§ 1542, 1418; in other systems of community, only when he is placed under guardianship as a spendthrift, *ibid.*, §§ 1468, 1549.

[6] Italy, C. C., 1441; Spain, C. C., 1433; Germany, in case of community of acquisitions, B. G., §§ 1542, 1418; Norway, Stat. June 29, 1888, art. 34.

[7] Germany, B. G., §§ 1468, 1542.

[8] Germany, B. G., § 1432; Saxony, B. G., § 1691; Austria, B. G., §§ 1217, 1263; Norway, Stat. June 29, 1888, art. 34; Switz., *Vorentwurf*, 195; for particular modifications in Prussia (A. L. R., ii, 1, §§ 354 *seq.*, 412 *seq.*), see *ante*, § 12, note 7.

[9] France, C. C., 1441; Spain, C. C., 72; Germany, B. G., § 1564 *seq.*; Prussia, A. L. R., ii, 1, § 732; Saxony, B. G., §§ 1706, 1712, 1740; Austria, B. G., § 1266; Basle, Stat. Mch. 10, 1884, arts. 23, 26; Switz., *Vorentwurf*, 173; Finland, Stat. Apl. 15, 1889, c. v, art. 19; La., C. C., 159.

[10] France, C. C., 1441; Spain, C. C., 73; Italy, C. C., 1441; Germany, B. G., § 1586; Saxony, if for life, B. G., § 1706; La., C. C., 155.

carry with it a dissolution of the community, but only the right to demand the same.[11]

(e) *As a Result of the Death of One of the Parties.*

The dissolution of the marriage by the death of either party has generally the effect of dissolving the matrimonial property relationships. This rule is subject to an exception in the case of general community, where issue of the marriage exists. In such event the community is continued (*fortgestzte Gütergemeinschaft; communauté prolongée*) between the surviving married party and the common children. This rule, which had its origin among the Westphalian Saxons,[12] seems to be the logical development of the strict principle of the general community. It has not, however, been generally accepted in modern legislations.[13] It obtains in localities in Germany and Switzerland, and the new code of Germany as well as the Swiss draft code have recognized the principle. In the former, such community arises by operation of law, but may be renounced by the surviving married party,[14] while in the latter the system must be the result of agreement between the survivor and the common children.[15]

In general, the continued community is subject to the same regulations as the general community of property between the married parties. The survivor possesses the

[11] Saxony, if separation is not to continue during life, B. G., § 1706; Austria, the innocent party may resist such demand, B. G., § 1264; Basle, Stat. Mch. 10, 1884, art. 22; Switzerland, if separation is to continue for one year or longer, *Vorentwurf*, 174.

[12] Heusler, *Inst.*, vol. ii, §§ 151, 162.

[13] France, C. C., 1441; Prussia, A. L. R., ii, 1, §§ 634–636; Saxony, B. G., § 1702; Austria, B. G., § 1234; Basle, Stat. Mch. 10, 1884, art. 13; a right of usufruct is granted survivor in portions falling by succession to share of common minor children, *ibid.*, art. 19.

[14] Germany, B. G., §§ 1483, 1484.

[15] Switz., *Vorentwurf*, 256.

rights and obligations of the husband, while the common
children occupy the legal position of the wife.[16]   The individual property owned by the common children does not fall
into the common mass.[17]   In Germany, all property acquired
by such children is likewise excluded, but the Swiss draft
code regards as their separate property only such acquisitions as come to them by gratuitous title.   The dissolution
of the community may be brought about by the act of the
survivor at any time.[18]   It results by operation of law in
case of the remarriage or death of such survivor,[19] and it
may be demanded by the children under the same general
conditions which entitle the wife to move for a separation of
property.[20]

§ 24. *Effects of the Dissolution of the Community.*

The dissolution of the community leads regularly to a
separation of property between the married parties or their
representatives.   The liquidation of the community proceeds in accordance with the principles determining rights
and obligations under the particular communal system.
The common obligations must be satisfied out of the joint
property.   If the latter does not suffice, the husband is
personally bound for all such obligations.[1]

The privilege which the wife enjoys of being relieved
from responsibility for all common debts, except those
which as between husband and wife fall to her charge,[2] is not

---

[16] Germany, B. G., § 1487; Switz., *Vorentwurf,* 257, 258.

[17] Germany, B. G., § 1485; Switz., *Vorentwurf,* 257.

[18] Germany, B. G., § 1492: Switz., *Vorentwurf,* 259.

[19] Germany, B. G., §§ 1493, 1494; Switz., and also in case of bankruptcy, *Vorentwurf,* 260.

[20] Germany, B. G., § 1495; *cf.* Switz., *Vorentwurf,* 259.

[1] For particular exceptions in France and Germany, see *ante,* § 19, note 8.

[2] *Ante,* § 19 (a).

always an absolute exemption. She is generally accorded
the right of obtaining such exemption by means of a renunciation or inventory, or both. According to the former, she
relieves herself from all liability by renouncing her share in
the common property.[3] The second method gives the wife
or her representatives the benefit of inventory which is generally accorded to the heirs of a succession. She is permitted, in accepting the community, to make an inventory
of the same, and in such case will be bound for the debts, as
regards creditors, as well as the husband or his representatives, only to the extent of the common property which she
receives.[4]

The German code gives the wife an absolute exemption
from personal liability for the obligations resulting from the
husband's administration of the community, and hence the
benefit of renunciation or inventory is unnecessary.[5] She will
be responsible, to the extent of the common property which
she receives, for such common debts as remain unsatisfied at
the time the separation of property is made.[6] The husband,
however, is subject to a warranty that the wife will not be
called upon to liquidate obligations which, as between the
parties, fall to his charge or to that of the common property,
and the wife is under similar obligation towards her husband
respecting debts falling to her charge.[7]

After the liquidation of the common obligations, the prop-

---

[3] France, C. C., 1453 *seq.*, 1492 *seq.;* Italy, C. C., 1444; Switz., *Vorentwurf,*
254; La., C.C., 2410, 2411.

[4] France, C. C., 1483; Italy, C. C., 1444; Prussia, privilege of inventory exists
for either party, A. L. R., ii, I, § 661, i, 9, § 418 *seq.;* Switz., *Vorentwurf,* 254;
La., C. C., 2413, 2414, 2419, 2423.

[5] B. G., § 1443; *cf.* Finland, Stat. Apl. 15, 1889, c. iv, arts. 2, 3; Basle, Stat. Mch.
10, 1884, art. 6; references to American statutes, *ante,* § 19, note 23.

[6] B. G., § 1480.

[7] *Ibid.,* § 1481; *cf.* Norway, Stat. June 29, 1888, art. 37.

erty is divided between the parties or their representatives.[8] Such amounts as have been paid out of the common mass to satisfy debts which are personal to either party are counted in the share of such party, and he is entitled to credit for such sums as have been paid out of his individual goods for the benefit of the common property.

Inasmuch as the common mass may contain articles of peculiar personal value to one of the parties, it is generally provided that such objects may be selected by the party before division, the value of the same being deducted from his share.[9]

If the conjugal association is not dissolved or suspended, the matrimonial property relations for the future will be regulated by the system of separate property.[10] On the other hand, where the community ceases as a result of the dissolution of the marriage, there is no further question of matrimonial property rights, and the parties or their representatives take their shares as strangers, subject to such particular qualifications as may be connected with the circumstances of the dissolution. Thus, special provisions exist for the case where the marriage is dissolved by decree of divorce. Privileges are generally accorded the innocent party over and above the right to receive support from the guilty party.[11]

[8] France, C. C., 1474; Spain, C. C., 1424, 1426; Germany, B. G., §§ 1476, 1546, 1549; Prussia, A. L. R., ii, 1, §§ 637, 638; Saxony, B. G., § 1702; Austria, B. G., § 1234; Finland, Stat. Apl. 15, 1889, c. i. art. 2 *seq.;* Switz., *Vorentwurf,* 253; La., C. C., 2406; for particular rule in some of the Swiss cantons, see *post,* notes. 13, 15, 16.

[9] Germany, B. G., § 1477; Prussia, without deduction from share in community, A. L. R., ii, 1, § 640, 641; Switz., *Vorentwurf,* 255.

[10] Germany, B. G., §1470; Prussia, A. L. R., ii, 1, §§ 392, 410; France, C. C., 1443 *seq.;* Switz., *Vorentwurf,* 197 *seq.*

[11] Germany, the right to demand that each shall receive the value of all the property that he brought into the common mass, any deficiency to be equally sustained

When the conjugal relation is dissolved by the death of one of the parties, the survivor takes one share of the common property and the succession of the deceased receives the other.[12] In some cases, however, rights of succession come in combination with pure matrimonial rights and affect the equality of the shares. Thus, in the canton of Basle City, the survivor takes two-thirds and the heirs of the decedent receive one-third of the common property.[13] The excess taken by the survivor is in the nature of a legal portion in the succession of the decedent.[14] Under the law existing before the enactment of the statute of 1884, the husband received two-thirds and the wife one-third.[15] This rule still obtains in some of the Swiss cantons.[16] In some of the American states, the surviving husband is entitled to the entire common property, while the surviving wife takes only a moiety.[17] The greater number of legislations, however, support the principle of division into equal parts, leaving the survivor to his general rights of succession in the estate of the decedent.[18]

by each party, B. G., § 1478; Prussia, A. L. R., ii, 1, §§ 755 seq., 812 seq.; Basle, Stat. Mch. 10, 1884, art. 23 seq.; Switz., Vorentwurf, 170; for rule in American community systems, cf. references, post, § 43, notes 13, 14.

[12] France, C. C., 1474; Germany, B. G., § 1482; Prussia, A. L. R., ii, 1, §§ 637, 638; Saxony, B. G., §1702; Austria, B. G., § 1234; Switz., Vorentwurf, 253.

[13] Stat. Mch. 10, 1884, art. 13.

[14] Post, § 47.

[15] Lardy, Législations Suisses, p. 51.

[16] See ibid., chart in appendix, showing attitude of cantons respecting this matter.

[17] Cal., C. C., §§ 1401, 1402; Idaho, R. S., 1887, §§ 5712, 5713; Nev., G. S., 1885, §§ 508, 509; for other particular regulations concerning succession to common property, see Prussia, A. L. R., ii, 1, § 638 seq.; Ariz., R. S., 1887, §§ 1100, 1467; Cal., C. C., § 1265; Idaho, R. S., 1887, §§ 3073, 5447; Texas, R. S., 1895, art. 1696; Wash., G. S., 1861, § 1481.

[18] Post, § 45 seq.

CHAPTER IV.

SYSTEMS OF INDIVIDUAL PROPERTY.

DIVISION I.

EXCLUSIVE RIGHTS OF THE HUSBAND.

§ 25. *In Roman and in Teutonic Law.*

The family relations in early Roman and in early Teutonic law were characterized by the element of paternal headship and authority. This was true as well of the relation between husband and wife as of that between parent and child. The Roman law was primarily influenced by the conception of the power and right of the man, while the Teutonic law emphasized the idea of guardianship in the position of the husband and father. In the Roman *manus* marriage, the wife, in the eyes of the law, occupied the position of a slave. This form of marriage may be regarded as a legal method of transferring ownership in the person and property of the woman. The woman occupied essentially the same legal relation toward her husband that she had formerly held with respect to her father or *pater familias*. The latter was master of the persons and goods of his household, so that there could arise no questions of personal or property rights between him and the members of his family. As regards third parties, the relations would be determined as in the case of master and slave. The property which the woman held or which was constituted for her benefit, passed into the possession or ownership of her husband. He became liable on her contracts in the same degree as if the obligations had

been contracted by his child or slave, and the same was true
of his responsibility for her tortious acts.[1] In this system
there were no proper matrimonial relations. The husband's
rights were paternal rather than marital, and, so far as the
law was concerned, paternal rights were as unlimited as those
of a *dominus.*

This rigorous system received modifications at an early
period. The extreme legal powers of the husband, which
resulted from his *manus,* were not necessarily embodied in
actual conditions. With the development of the free marriage, where *manus mariti* was excluded, the property as
well as the personal rights of the wife came to be recognized. The woman in contracting marriage did not lose her
position in her agnatic family, and hence did not suffer a
diminution in her status. The exclusive property rights of
the husband disappeared with the loss of his absolute powers
over the person of his wife. The marriage, as such, did not
affect the property of the woman. This did not exclude
property relations between husband and wife. Strictly
speaking, such relations were now for the first time recognized. They resulted, however, not directly from the establishment of the conjugal relation, but from specific acts of
the parties or of persons acting in their behalf.[2]

In Teutonic law the domination of the man was not immediately connected with conceptions of power and force.
The element of guardianship was the characteristic feature.
Primitive law, however, emphasized the rights instead of the
duties of the guardian. By the marriage, the woman, with
her property, passed from the control of her father to that
of her husband. Whether the latter became the owner of
such property is a disputed question.[3] Where the *Raubehe*

[1] Sohm, *Inst.,* §§ 93, 94; Muirhead, *Roman Law,* p. 27.

[2] Sohm, *Inst.,* §§ 93, 94.

[3] Heusler, *Inst.,* vol. ii, pp. 294 *seq.,* 303 *seq.;* Schröder, *Lehrbuch,* p. 304, n. 196.

was the typical form of marriage, there could be no question
of legal property relations between the parties.   This was
not necessarily true of the *Brautkauf*, and it is clear that at
an early period certain property was recognized as belonging to the wife.[4]   The husband, as the guardian of the wife,
continued to administer such property.

The development was influenced by local conditions, as a
result of which distinct types appeared.   Upon one side, the
Germanic conception of society or partnership found expression in various forms of community of property.   On the
other hand, the principle that the wife or some one acting
for her should make a contribution to support the common
expenses was embodied in the systems of marital usufruct.

The English common law represents a type of the system
of exclusive rights of the husband, though particular modifications, in derogation of the general principle, are to be noted.[5]
The husband is entitled to the sole administration of all of
the wife's property.   All of the personal property which he
brings into his possession, becomes his property.   For the
real property the principle of marital administration and
usufruct obtains.   The husband cannot affect the substance
of such property, but he is entitled to the income and profits
and is not required to account for the same.   In addition,
the husband has the right to his wife's services and to all
that she may acquire by her personal activity.   Connected
with these extensive privileges is his liability for the wife's
obligations, whether arising in contract or in tort.[6]

---

[4] The wife brings with her a species of dowry (*Gerade*); the husband makes
certain gifts to the wife, *e. g.*, the *dos*, which Tacitus describes, *Morgengabe*, etc.

[5] It does not follow that these arose as limitations upon the absolute powers of
the husband.   Quite the converse may have been true.   They may be the remains
of a system which accorded the wife greater rights, of which a later period deprived
her; *cf.* Pol. & Mait., *Hist.*, vol. ii, pp. 400, 401.

[6] Pol. & Mait., *Hist.*, vol. ii., pp. 401–403.

The dower of the wife and the curtesy of the husband were distinguishing features of the common law system. By the beginning of the thirteenth century, the principle was established that a widow is entitled to an estate for life in one-third of all the lands of which the husband is seized of an estate of inheritance during the marriage. The husband could not limit this privilege of the wife, and it was not subject to the claims of his creditors. While primarily intended as a provision for the widow, it was something more than a mere right of succession. The wife acquired a form of proprietary right in her husband's lands. While she could not make good her claims during the marriage, they would attach so as to enable her, upon the death of her husband, to follow lands which he may have alienated during the marriage, without her consent, given in the formal manner required.[7]

The husband, upon the birth of issue of the marriage, became entitled to a tenancy by the curtesy, for his life, in all of the lands of which the wife was seized during coverture. The effect of the fulfillment of the condition was to extend the husband's interest in the wife's lands from an estate for their joint lives to an estate for his life.[8]   It is somewhat analogous to the continued community, where the matrimonial property relations are practically unaffected by the dissolution of the marriage so long as one of the parties survives. In effect, the husband's guardianship of the matrimonial property was extended so as to apply, during his life, to the share falling to the issue of the marriage. It is necessary to note, however, that while the birth of such issue was essential to the extension of such guardianship, the latter continued, notwithstanding the fact that no issue survived at the death of his wife.

[7] *Ibid.*, p. 418 *seq.*   [8] *Ibid.*, p. 412 *seq.*

These are the fundamental features of the common law matrimonial property system which obtained in England and was carried over into the legal systems of most of the American states. It was adapted to a rude state of society, where personal property was of little consequence. With the increasing importance of the latter, the hardships of the system made themselves manifest, and remedial measures became necessary.[9]

DIVISION II.

MARITAL ADMINISTRATION AND USUFRUCT.

§ 26. *General Character of the Wife's Property.*

The general principle at the basis of the system of marital administration and usufruct is that, as a result of the marriage, the property which the woman possesses and that which she afterwards acquires pass into the administration of the husband, who is entitled to the use and proceeds of the same. The title to such property remains in the wife.[1] Thus, by operation of law, the property of the married woman becomes dotal in character.

An exception to the general rule arises in the recognition that certain kinds of property are excluded from the husband's control and enjoyment, and are reserved for the administration and usufruct of the wife. The character of the system and the position of the wife with respect to her

---

[9] See *post*, § 37.

[1] Germany, B. G., § 1363; Prussia, A. L. R.. ii, 1, § 200; Saxony, B. G., § 1655; France, C. C., 1529 *seq.*; Glaris, L. B., ii, art. 172; Lucerne, Stat. Nov. 26, 1880, art. 6; Zürich, P. R. G., §§ 589, 593; Switz., *Vorentwurf*, 226 *seq.* In a few of the Swiss legislations the husband becomes owner of the wife's fortune, and is responsible for its value (Lardy, *Législations Suisses*, pp. 27, 65). In many cantons his unlimited powers of disposition produce practically the same result (*cf. post*, § 27, note 2).

property will be affected by the extent of the separate[2] property which obtains.

Separate property may arise as a result of contract between the parties,[3] by the act of a third party, where property accrues to the wife by donation or succession, and the donor or testator provides that it shall become her separate property,[4] or by operation of law. While the two former sources may lead to a wide extension of separate property, it is the last which is of chief importance in determining the general property rights of married women under any particular system.

The legislations, in general, accord the character of statutory separate property to all things which are intended for the sole personal use of the wife.[5] According to the three preliminary drafts of the code of Germany such objects were dotal property (*Ehegut*), but were excluded from the marital usufruct.[6] Thus, the husband could control the disposition of such property.[7] In the code, as finally adopted, this position was rejected. The articles are in-

---

[2] In the consideration of systems of individual property the terms "dotal" and "separate" property are used in the same sense as that previously indicated under systems of community. Under individual systems, however, the proceeds of dotal property go to the husband alone. *Cf. ante,* §15.

[3] Germany, B. G., § 1368; Prussia, A. L. R., ii, 1, § 208; Saxony, B. G., §§ 1691, 1693; France, C C., 1387; Lucerne, but cannot exceed one-third of the fortune of the wife, Stat. Nov. 26, 1880, art. 11; Zürich, P. R. G., § 597; Switz., *Vorentwurf,* 216; *cf. ante,* § 12.

[4] Germany, B. G,, § 1369; Prussia, A. L. R., ii, 1, § 214; Saxony, B. G., § 1693; France, C. C., 1401; Lucerne, Stat. Nov. 26, 1880, art. 11; Glaris, L. B., ii, art. 174; Zürich, P. R. G., § 597; Switz., *Vorentwurf,* 216.

[5] Germany, B. G., § 1366; Prussia, A. L. R., ii, 1, § 206; Saxony. B. G., § 1671; Lucerne, Stat. Nov. 26, 1880, art. 11; Glaris, L. B., ii, art. 174; Zürich, P. R. G., § 597; Switz., *Vorentwurf,* 217.

[6] I. *Entwurf,* § 1285; II. *Entwurf,* § 1282; III. *Entwurf,* § 1354.

[7] In Saxony the husband could prevent the wife from making any other than the intended use of such objects. B. G., § 1671.

cluded in the statutory separate property of the married woman, and, as such, are subject to the exclusive administration as well as the enjoyment of the wife.[8] Statutory reserved property also includes the things accruing from or taken in exchange or as compensation for separate property.[9]

Under individual systems, the principle that the husband has an exclusive right to the services, and hence to all of the personal acquisitions of his wife, is apt to entail greater hardships than it produces in systems recognizing a community of property interests. Under a strict application of the principle, all that the wife acquires by her industry would become the husband's sole property. The legislations have, therefore, generally modified the rule so as to secure to the wife an interest in the products of her personal activity. In the more recent legislations this has been accomplished by giving the character of statutory separate property to that which is the result of her labor or is acquired in a business which she carries on independently of her husband.[10] The older codes, however, regard such property as dotal property, the capital of which is preserved for the wife, while the husband has the use of the same.[11]

[8] B. G., §§ 1366, 1371, 1427 *seq.*

[9] Germany, B. G., § 1370; Prussia, A. L. R., ii, 1, § 217; Saxony, B. G., § 1693; Lucerne, Stat. Nov. 26, 1880, art. 12.

[10] Germany, B. G., § 1367; Lucerne, Stat. Nov. 26, 1880, art. 11; Zürich, limited to that which she acquires in an independent occupation or industry, but includes capital as well as profits so long as such activity is continued, P. R. G., § 621, 622; Switzerland, all property employed in business become separate property, *Vorentwurf*, 217.

[11] Prussia, A. L. R., ii, 1, § 220; if business is transacted entirely with her separate property, the income will have the same character, *ibid.*, § 219; Saxony, B. G., § 1668. In many of the Swiss cantons the husband becomes owner of the property which the wife acquires by her personal industry: Glaris, L. B., ii, art. 173; Zürich, so far as it is not acquired in an independent occupation, P. R. G., § 593; *cf.* Lardy, *Législations Suisses*, pp. 8, 17, 27, 65, 175, 204, 277, 299, 303, 347.

§ 27. *Administration of the Wife's Property.*

The husband is the administrator of the dotal or matrimonial property. He is entitled to take possession of it and to exercise all functions connected with its ordinary administration. To this extent, there is general agreement among the codes. Marked divergence appears, however, respecting the further extension of his powers, and particularly with reference to his right to dispose of the property. Many of the Swiss cantons emphasize the exclusive rights of the husband. In some cases he becomes owner of the wife's property subject to the obligation to return its value.[1] In other instances he is given an absolute right of disposing of all of the dotal property subject to the same liability.[2] The wife or her representatives will receive the value of the property which she has brought into the marriage without any deduction for the losses, or any claim to a share in the gains which have accrued.[3]

The German systems and the Swiss draft code, however, start with the general principle that the wife's property shall be kept intact, and that the husband shall not dispose of the substance of the same nor bind it in any way without the consent of the wife.[4] The rule is similar to that which governs the relations between the owner and usufructuary in an ordinary usufruct. This principle, however, is not rigorously maintained in the case of the ordinary usufructuary, and it is naturally modified in the interests of the marital administra-

----

[1] *Ante*, § 26, note 1.

[2] Glaris, L. B., ii, arts. 172, 177; *cf.* Lucerne, Stat. Nov. 26. 1880, arts. 5–7; Lardy, *Législations Suisses*, pp. 8, 17, 125, 176, 204, 217, 293, 303.

[3] *Contra* in Glaris, where the wife is entitled to profit upon sales of her property. She also suffers the losses in such cases if husband proves that same are not due to his fault. L. B., ii, art. 177.

[4] Germany, B. G., § 1375; Prussia, A. L. R., ii, 1, § 231 *seq.*; Saxony, B. G., §§660 623; Switz., *Vorentwurf*, 230.

tion. So far as immovables are concerned, the general rule is maintained that they cannot be alienated or encumbered without the consent of the wife.[5]

It is with respect to the disposition of movables that the codes begin to differ. Some accord the husband the general right of disposition, limited, of course, by his obligation to restore the value of the objects alienated.[6] Others tend to make the right of disposition as limited as that possessed by an ordinary usufructuary.[7] Important considerations are connected with the determination of this matter. The free activity of the husband may be required in the interests of the matrimonial property. The interests of the wife, on the other hand, may necessitate protection against the acts of the husband affecting the substance of such property. It is undesirable, moreover, to adopt provisions that may encourage legal proceedings between married parties. Finally, the power of disposition must not be of such a character as to deceive third parties.

The first draft of the German code placed chief stress upon the husband's right of usufruct. It did not treat his right of administration as a personal right resulting from the

[5] Germany, B. G., § 1375; Prussia, A. L. R., ii, 1, § 232; Saxony, B. G., § 660; France, C. C., 1428; Lucerne, Stat. Nov. 26, 1880, art. 7; Zürich, P. R. G., § 591; Switz., *Vorentwurf*, 230; *cf.* Lardy, *Législations Suisses*, pp. 39, 87, 278, 348.

[6] Prussia, A. L. R., ii, 1, § 247, but not of capital invested in the name of the wife, or of her donor or testator, *ibid.*, § 233; France, C. C., 1531, 1532; Lucerne, if by ante-nuptial contract this right of disposition is restricted, the titles of ownership of the wife must be publicly registered, Stat. Nov. 26, 1880, art. 6; Zürich, P. R. G., § 590; *cf.* § 592.

[7] Saxony, B. G., §§ 660, 1655, 1674, 1677; Lardy, *Législations Suisses*, p. 277. The Swiss draft code provides that the husband cannot dispose, without the wife's consent, of any of the marital property, of which he has not acquired the ownership. It raises a presumption of the consent of the wife for the benefit of innocent third parties, except where it should have been clear to every one that the property belongs to the wife (*Vorentwurf*, 230). If husband has given security for the movables he may freely dispose of the same (*ibid.*, 231).

establishment of the marriage relation, but defined it independently and limited it to very narrow bounds. Emphasis
was placed upon the fact that he was the administrator of
property of which the title was in another person. Hence
for all important acts of administration he must act with the
authorization of such party, and in the name of the latter.[8] It
was expressly provided that the general rules governing the
administration of property subjected to a usufruct, should
apply to the husband's usufruct in the matrimonial property,
except where the code provided otherwise.[9] So, also, his
powers of disposition were limited to the alienation of objects
whose use in general consisted in their consumption,[10] and to
such acts, in the name of the wife, as were necessary to fulfill
obligations binding upon the dotal property.[11] For all other
acts of disposition he must have the authorization of the wife
to act in her name.[12]

These provisions of the draft code became the subject of
severe criticism on the part of those who conceived that the
establishment of the property relations between husband and
wife, upon the same basis as that existing between an owner
and a usufructuary, was contrary to the true conception of
the conjugal relationship. They insisted that the husband's
right was something more than that of a simple usufructuary; that his right of administration flowed directly from
the personal relation which the marriage established, and
was not a mere incident of his right of usufruct. It was
argued that the provisions of the draft code would tend to
the detriment of the matrimonial property, and that the
right of either party to maintain judicial proceedings against
the other, for claims arising out of the marital administra-

[8] I. *Entwurf*, §§ 1317–1325.

[9] *Ibid.*, § 1292.   [10] *Ibid.*, § 1294.

[11] *Ibid*, § 1318.   [12] *Ibid*, § 1319.

tion, would lead to conflicts between the husband and wife which would destroy the family unity.[13]

These arguments had weight, and in the later drafts and the code as finally adopted, the husband's right of administration is regarded as a direct outgrowth of the matrimonial relationship.[14] By virtue of the marriage the husband acquires the personal right of administering the dotal property, though in the interests of the wife, this general right is limited by important exceptions, A middle ground is taken between the two extreme views respecting the husband's right to dispose of the dotal property. The positive acts that he can perform without the consent of his wife include those recognized in the first draft code, and in addition, the right to dispose of money and other consumable objects. The latter include things whose customary use is exchange or alienation, *e. g.*, a stock of goods, as well as those whose customary use lies in their consumption.[15] Moreover, the husband disposes of such objects in his own name, and he can legally enforce in the same manner all rights connected with the dotal property.[16] If the matter is one over which he can dispose without the assistance of his wife, the judgment in such process will be binding upon her. On the other hand, the husband is not permitted to dispose of other movables without the consent of the wife,[17] but, following the

[13] Brühl, "Die eheliche Nutzniessung," *Arch. f. d. civ. Prax.*, vol. 73, p. 408 *seq.*; Gierke, *Entwurf*, pp. 409, 410, 412–414; Mitteis, "Bemerkungen zum ehelichen Güterrecht," *Zeit. f. d. Privat. u. öff. Recht.*, vol. 16, pp. 545, 582.

[14] II. *Entwurf*, §§ 1272–1293; III. *Entwurf*, §§ 1356–1377; B. G.: §§ 1373–1394.

[15] Germany, B. G. §§ 1376, 92; *cf.* Switz., *Vorentwurf*, 229.

[16] Germany, B. G. § 1380.

[17] The second and third drafts of the code permitted the husband to collect non-interest bearing demands without the consent of his wife (II. *Entwurf*, § 1275; III. *Entwurf*, § 1359), but this provision was stricken out in the final revision.

practice of other systems, it is provided that such consent may be supplied by the court when it is refused on insufficient grounds, or when the absence or illness of the wife prevents her from giving her consent.[18]   Finally, it is necessary to note that the personal character of the husband's right of administration and usufruct is emphasized by his inability to alienate his right as such.[19]

The husband's power of administration is protected against interference on the part of the wife.   The latter has no general right of disposition over the dotal property.   She is prevented from encumbering or otherwise disposing of the same, by virtue of her general incapacity to contract without the marital authorization,[20] or in those systems which recognize the general contractual capacity of married women, by positive provisions making such dispositions dependent upon the consent of the husband.[21]   The dispositions made without the husband's consent are ineffective so far as regards the dotal property, but they may be binding upon the wife's separate property.

The wife is not entirely excluded from acts of administration or disposition over the dotal property.   She may bind the latter within the sphere of her activity as administrator of the domestic affairs of the household,[22] or in an independent business which she carries on with the consent of her husband.[23]   The wife does not require the marital

[18] Germany, B. G., § 1379; *cf.* Prussia, A. L. R. ii. 1, § 299; Saxony, B. G., § 1657.

[19] Germany, B. G., § 1408.

[20] *Ante*, § 3.

[21] Germany, B. G., § 1395; Prussia, A. L. R. ii. 1, § 320; Saxonv, B. G., § 1638; Switz., *Vorentwurf,* 232.

[22] *Ante*, § 8.

[23] *Ante*, § 6; Germany, B. G., § 1405; Prussia, A. L. R. ii. 1, §§ 335–337; France, C. C., 220; Lucerne, Stat. Nov. 26, 1880, art. 17; Zürich. P. R. G., §§ 621, 622; Glaris, L. B. ii., art. 175.

authorization for the acceptance or rejection of gifts or successions which fall to her,[24] or for the carrying on of certain judicial processes for the protection of her rights.[25] Where other acts of the wife are necessary, the court may supply the consent of the husband if it is refused without sufficient reason.[26] Such acts may also be performed by the wife without the consent of the husband where the latter on account of illness or absence is prevented from manifesting his will and there is risk of damage from delay.[27]

The property which is reserved for the wife under the system of marital administration and usufruct, is subject to the same rules of administration as obtain for the wife's property, in general, under the system of separate property.[28]

§ 28. *Liability for Debts.*

The husband enjoys the fruits of the matrimonial property and he is accordingly subject to the obligations of a usufructuary. As such, he must defray the costs of administration, and meet the public and private obligations which are binding upon the dotal property.[1] He is not under a general obligation to answer for the debts of his wife, his liability being connected with his relation to the matrimonial property rather than his personal relation to his wife. The husband is under a personal obligation to support the

---

[24] Germany, B. G., § 1406; *contra*, Switz., *Vorentwurf*, 232.

[25] Germany, B. G., §1407.

[26] Germany, B. G., § 1402; Saxony, B. G., §1644; France, C. C., 218, 219; Switz., *Vorentwurf*, 232.

[27] Germany, B. G., § 1401; Prussia, A. L. R., ii, 1, §§ 202–204, 326, 327; Saxony, B. G., § 1643; *cf.* France, C. C., 1427.

[28] *Post*, § 42.

[1] Germany, B. G., §§ 1383–1388; Prussia, A. L. R., ii, 1, § 231; Saxony, B. G., § 660; France, C. C., 1533; Lucerne, Stat., Nov. 26, 1880, art. 13; Glaris, L. B., ii, art. 176; Switz., *Vorentwurf*, 228, 232.

family,² and he may be liable for debts which the wife contracts for this purpose.³

While the husband is under no general liability for the debts of the wife, the dotal property, of which he has the usufruct, is subject to such charges.⁴ This liability does not extend to obligations arising from post-nuptial contracts of the wife, made without the necessary consent of the husband,⁵ or which have been incurred in the administration of her separate property.⁶ The creditors, in such cases, can hold the dotal property, during the continuance of the marital usufruct, only to the extent to which such property has been enriched by the act.⁷

As between the married parties, compensation is due from the separate property to the dotal property, when the latter is diminished by reason of the payments of obligations arising from torts or unlawful acts committed by the wife.⁸ The same is true when the wife's expenses in a judicial pro-

---

² Germany, B. G., § 1389; Prussia, A. L. R., ii, 1, §§ 185 *seq.*, 321; Saxony, B. G., §§ 1634, 1635; France, C. C., 1530; Lucerne, Stat., Nov. 26, 1880, art. 2; Glaris, L. B., ii, arts. 169, 170.

³ *Ante*, § 8. In the German code it is provided that the wife may demand that the net income of the dotal property, so far as it may be necessary for the support of the family, shall be applied to that purpose without regard to the other obligations of the husband, B. G., § 1389; *cf.* Zürich, P. R. G., § 594.

⁴ Germany, B. G., § 1411; Prussia, A. L. R., ii, 1, § 338; Saxony, B. G., § 1679; Glaris, L. B., ii, art. 176; Lucerne, Stat., Nov. 26, 1880, art. 13; Switz., *Vorentwurf*, 233, 235.

⁵ *Ante*, § 27.

⁶ Germany, unless they arise out of an independent business which she carries on with husband's consent, B. G., §§ 1413, 1414; Prussia, A. L. R., ii, 1, § 229; Saxony, B. G., § 1640.

⁷ Germany, B. G., § 1399; Lucerne, Stat., Nov. 26, 1880, art. 13; Glaris, L. B., ii, art. 175.

⁸ Germany, B. G., § 1415; Saxony, B. G., § 1680; *cf.* Prussia, A. L. R., ii, 1, §§ 339, 340.

ceeding with her husband are defrayed out of the dotal property.[9]

§ 29. *Protection of the Wife's Property.*

In addition to the limitations placed upon the administration of the husband, the legislations generally provide special means for the protection of the property rights of the married woman. The presumption, which is raised in favor of creditors, that existing movables belong to the husband,[1] may be rebutted by an inventory.[2] It is also recognized that the wife may demand that the husband shall furnish particular security for the property of which he has the administration.[3] While the states generally give the wife all the rights of an ordinary creditor of the husband, some legislations go further, and concede her a right of registering a mortgage in her favor over the immovables of the husband,[4] or accord her special privileges in the latter's bankruptcy.[5] Where these privileges exist, the husband's right

[9] Germany, same principle applies to costs of legal proceedings in general, B. G., § 1416; Saxony, B. G., § 1681.

[1] *Ante*, § 5.

[2] Germany, B. G., § 1372; Glaris, L. B., ii, art. 177; Lucerne, Stat., Nov. 26, 1880, arts. 8-10; Zürich, P. R. G., § 604; *cf.* Prussia, A. L. R., ii, 1, § 544; Saxony, B. G., § 1656; Austria, B. G., § 1237; France, C. C., 1532.

[3] Only when her rights are endangered: Germany, B. G., §§ 1391–1393; Prussia, A. L. R., ii, 1, § 255; Lucerne, Stat., Nov. 26, 1880, art. 18; at any time: Zürich, P. R. G., § 604 *seq.;* Switz., *Vorentwurf,* 213.

[4] Prussia, A. L. R., ii, 1, § 254, limited to one year from beginning of husband's administration, Stat. of May 8, 1855, G. S. S., p. 317; Saxony, B. G., § 390; *cf.* France, C. C., 2135, 1540.

[5] Glaris, L. B., ii, art. 178; Lucerne, Stat., Nov. 26, 1880, art. 23; Zürich, P. R. G., § 611; Lardy, *Législations Suisses,* pp. 9, 27, 40, 66, 176, 217, 292, 303, 348. The Swiss federal law of bankruptcy places the wife, where her privilege is recognized by cantonal law, in the fourth class of creditors, but the privileged share of her property cannot exceed one-half, Alexander, *Konk.-G.,* p. 307. A similar privilege, recognized in Prussia (A. L. R., ii, 1, § 259; *Konk. Ordnung,* § 80, G. S. S., 1855, p. 321), was abrogated when the imperial law of bankruptcy was introduced in 1877 (*Konk. Ordnung,* § 54, R. G. Bl., pp. 351, 362).

of administration is generally quite extensive, and the tendency is for them to disappear as limitations are placed upon the husband's power. While affording adequate protection to the wife, they constitute a serious detriment to the marital administration and a menace to the interests of third parties.

The final remedy, which the wife possesses for the protection of her property interests, is her right to demand that the marital administration and usufruct be terminated. In the new code of Germany, this power, and the privilege of demanding security when her rights are endangered,[6] are made more effective by the fact that the husband is under an obligation to render the wife a statement of the condition of the administration of the dotal property.[7]

§ 30. *Termination of the Marital Administration and Usufruct.*

(a) *As the Legal Result of Bankruptcy.*

The system of marital administration and usufruct does not recognize any community of property interests between the married parties. It is indeed to meet the matrimonial expenses that the husband has the use of the wife's property; but in case he falls into bankruptcy, his personal creditors acquire a claim upon the fruits of such property and may thus defeat the ends for which it was established. Accordingly, the more recent legislations recognize that the bankruptcy of the husband has the legal effect of terminating his administration and usufruct of the dotal property.[1]

---

[6] *Ante*, note 3.

[7] Germany, B. G., §1374.

[1] Germany, B. G., § 1419; Switz., bankruptcy of either party, *Vorentwurf*, 197. Until the settlement of the bankruptcy or satisfaction of creditors: Lucerne, Stat., Nov. 26, 1880, art. 19; Zürich, P. R. G., § 613.

(b) *Upon the Demand of the Wife.*

The existing legislations generally agree in recognizing that the bankruptcy of the husband or irregularities in his administration of the dotal property justify the wife in demanding the termination of the marital administration and usufruct.[2] The failure of the husband to fulfill his statutory obligation to provide for the support of the family is also a valid ground for such demand.[3] The fact that the husband is under guardianship has also been recognized by the German code as sufficient ground for the demand for a cessation of the marital administration and usufruct, but the attainment of full capacity by the husband will enable him to demand the restoration of his marital property rights.[4]

The legislations do not recognize that the husband has the right to demand the dissolution of the matrimonial property relations where the marital administration and usufruct obtain.[5]

(c) *By Mutual Agreement.*

Where post-nuptial marriage agreements are not prohibited, the termination of the marital administration and usufruct may be brought about by agreement between the parties, subject to the observance of such formalities as the law may provide to safeguard the rights of third parties.[6]

[2] Germany, B. G., § 1418; Prussia, A. L. R., ii, 1, § 258; France, C. C., 1443; Glaris, L. B., ii, art. 179; Lucerne, Stat., Nov. 26, 1880, art. 18; Zürich, P. R. G., § 594; Switz., *Vorentwurf*, 198. In Saxony, the wife may demand that the administration shall be given to her. This will not affect husband's right of usufruct, B. G., §§ 1684, 1685; *cf. ante*, § 22, notes 9, 10.

[3] Germany, B. G., § 1418; Prussia, A. L. R., ii, 1, §§ 256, 258; Switz., *Vorentwurf*, 198; Lucerne, Stat., Nov. 26, 1880, art. 19; Zürich, P. R. G., § 594.

[4] B. G., §§ 1418, 1425; *cf.* Lucerne, Stat., Nov. 26, 1880, art. 20, Zürich, P. R. G., § 614.

[5] *Motive*, vol. iv, p. 294; Prussia, A. L. R., ii, 1, § 251; Saxony, B. G., § 1686; France, C. C., 1443; *contra*, Switz., *Vorentwurf*, 199.

[6] Germany, B. G., § 1435; Prussia, A. L. R., ii, 1, §§ 251, 252; Switz., *Vorentwurf*, 195; *cf.* Saxony, B. G., § 1694.

(d) *By the Dissolution of the Marriage.*

The dissolution of the marriage by the death of one of the parties or by decree of divorce leads regularly to a cessation of the marital administration and usufruct.[7] No provisions exist for a continuation of the property relations between the surviving married party and the common children.

§ 31. *Effects of the Termination of the Marital Administration and Usufruct.*

The general rule is that, upon the termination of the marital administration and usufruct, the dotal property is to be immediately returned to the wife or her representatives, in accordance with the regulations governing the ordinary usufruct.[1] The property, so far as it still exists, is to be returned,[2] and compensation must be rendered for the remainder, except where it has been destroyed without fault on the part of the husband.

The codes differ with respect to the compensation due the husband on account of expenditures which he has incurred for the dotal property, over and above those which he is legally obliged to sustain. The older codes require that these expenditures shall have been made with the consent of the wife.[3] If the husband has made the expenditure with-

---

[7] Regarding effects of judicial separation, see *ante*, § 23, (d).   Lucerne, Stat., Nov. 26, 1880, art. 19.

[1] Germany, B. G., §§ 1421, 1423; Prussia, A. L. R., ii. 1, §§ 548 *seq.*; 559 *seq.*; 570 *seq.*; 585 *seq.*; 595 *seq.*; interest can be demanded only after the expiration of the first quarter, if usufruct is terminated by death of either party, *ibid.*, § 549; Saxony, B. G., §§ 1688, 1689, 660; Glaris, L. B., ii, art. 177; Lucerne, Stat., Nov. 26, 1880, art. 21; Zürich, P. R. G., § 609.

[2] In Prussia, in case the marital usufruct ceases as a result of the death of the wife, the husband had an election between returning the real estate or its value, A. L. R., ii, 1, § 570 *seq.*

[3] Prussia, A. L. R., ii, 1, §§ 587, 588; Saxony, B. G., § 1690.

out the consent of the wife or the authorization of the court, he will be treated as an ordinary usufructuary and entitled to take back the improvements in so far as this is possible without producing alterations in the previous condition of the property.[4] The new German code adopts a more liberal attitude. It regards the husband, where he was justified in considering the expenditure necessary, as occupying the same position as one acting under a mandate, and as such entitled to compensation.[5]

If the conjugal community is not suspended or dissolved, the matrimonial property relations for the future will be regulated by the system of separate property.[6]

The legislations are divided regarding the effects of divorce upon property rights. Some do not accord any privilege to the innocent party aside from a claim to support,[7] while others recognize the right to demand particular compensation.[8] Where the marriage is dissolved as a result of the death of one of the parties, the dotal property will be returned to the wife or go over to her estate in succession.

[4] Prussia, A. L. R., ii, 1, § 586, i, 21, §§ 124–131; according to the code of Saxony he would be treated as one acting without a mandate and hence entitled to compensation to the extent to which the property was enriched, B. G., § 1690; cf. Lucerne, Stat., Nov. 26, 1880, art. 21.

[5] B. G., § 1390; cf. ibid., § 670.

[6] Germany, B. G., § 1426; France, C. C.. 1443 seq., 1449; Lucerne, Stat., Nov. 26, 1880, art. 22; Switz., Vorentwurf, 197 seq.; contra, Prussia, where existing system continues with the wife as administratrix and usufructuary, subject to the same obligations as were imposed upon the husband, A. L. R., ii, 1, §§ 258, 261 seq.; cf. Saxony, B. G., §§ 1684, 1685. In Zürich the dotal property will be administered under control of the court of guardians, P. R. G., § 594.

[7] Motive, vol. iv, p. 228 seq.; Germany, B. G., §§ 1578–1585; Saxony, B. G., § 1750.

[8] Prussia, A. L. R., ii, 1, § 766 seq.; France, C. C., 299 seq.; Lucerne, Stat., Nov. 26, 1880, art. 25; Switz., Vorentwurf, 170.

DIVISION III.

SYSTEM OF DOWRY.

§ 32. *General Character of the Wife's Property.*

The general principle at the basis of the system of dowry, as it is defined in the law of Justinian and in modern legislations, is that the marriage, as such, does not affect the legal proprietary relations of the parties. Nevertheless, the establishment of the conjugal relation, by producing certain effects upon the personal relations of the parties,[1] may exercise an influence upon their property rights. Moreover, the marriage regularly leads to other legal acts that result in the establishment of matrimonial property relations. The most important of these acts is the constitution of the dowry and the establishment of certain benefits for the wife.

The early Roman law of dowry was subjected to profound modifications as a result of juristic and legislative activity. Modern Roman law, however, exhibits distinct traces of its development from the primitive system. The dowry is primarily a contribution which the wife, or some one acting in her interest, makes to the husband to assist him in fulfilling his obligation of supporting the expenses of the matrimonial community.[2] In the second place, the dowry is intended as a means of future provision for the wife, and, as such, is to be preserved and returned to her upon the dissolution of the marriage.[3] This latter characteristic of the dowry was not recognized in the older Roman law. Custom led to its gradual introduction and establishment. The husband in some cases was bound by an express agreement to return the dowry. In other instances the wife was granted an *actio*

[1] *Cf. ante*, §§ 4, 5.

[2] Austria, B. G., § 1218; France, C. C., 1540; Italy, C. C., 1388; La., C. C., 2335.

[3] *Post*, § 36.

rei uxoriæ, under which the husband, while not bound in law to return the dowry, could be compelled to act in accordance with the principles of equity and good faith.[4] At a later period, imperial legislation completed the development by making provision for the preservation of the dowry during the period of the husband's administration, and by enabling the wife to maintain a personal action against the husband for the return of the same or to sue as owner of the dotal effects.[5]

The marriage does not give the husband a right to demand a dowry.[6] The latter is not established by the law as in the system of marital administration and usufruct. The dotal property, under the system of dowry, must have been given or promised to the husband.[7] The legal rules govern the dotal relation only after it has been established by the act of the parties or of persons acting in their interest.

While the dowry was not an essential feature of the marriage relation, it was, nevertheless, the general custom during the Roman period, for the woman to bring her husband a *dos*. An unendowed wife was apt to be regarded as resting under a stigma, an attitude which obtains to-day in some European countries. Thus, the Roman law and some European systems recognize that the daughter has a legal right to demand a dowry from her father or parents.[8]

---

[4] Sohm, *Inst.*, § 95.   [5] See *post*, §§ 33, 34.

[6] Windscheid, *Pandekten*, vol. ii, § 493; Dernburg, *Pandekten*, vol. iii, § 15.

[7] France, C. C., 1540, 1543; Italy, C. C., 1388, 1391; Spain, C. C., 1336; La., C. C., 2338; Austria, B. G., §§ 1218 *seq.*, 1225. In Austria, under the influence of the German principles of marital administration and usufruct, the presumption obtains, so long as the wife does not contradict it, that she has entrusted her husband with the administration of her property, and in this case, he is entitled to the fruits and profits. But his right ceases from the moment the wife manifests her opposition. *Ibid.*, §§ 1238, 1239.

[8] Windscheid, *Pandekten*, vol. ii, § 493; Dernburg, *Pandekten*, vol. iii, § 15; Austria, B. G., § 1220; Spain, C. C., 1340; *cf.* Saxony, B. G., § 1661 *seq.*; Germany, B. G., § 1620.

The Roman law developed side by side with the *dos*, the *donatio propter nuptias*.[9] This is a gift from the husband to the wife, intended as a future provision for the latter and made to take effect upon the dissolution of the marriage. The wife, in the free marriage at Roman law, had only a distant limited right of succession.[10] The *donatio propter nuptias* was a settlement which mitigated the hardships resulting from the law of succession as well as from the institution of free divorce. The Austrian civil code, under the title *Widerlage*, regulates a similar settlement for the wife.[11] In most of the modern codes, however, there is no special definition, the husband being permitted to make gifts to the wife, in augmentation of her dowry, subject to the rules regulating donations and agreements between married parties.[12]

All of the property of the wife, including the proceeds of her personal industry, which is not settled as part of her dowry, is her separate property (paraphernalia), and is in general subject to the provisions which regulate the wife's fortune under the system of separate property.[13]

§ 33. *Administration of the Dowry.*

As the dowry is constituted for the primary purpose of assisting the husband in sustaining the matrimonial charges, its administration must be directed to this end. The husband is therefore entitled to the administration of the dotal property. The extent of his rights in this respect was considerably limited in the course of Roman legal development. In the earliest period, the *dos*, in passing into the possession of the husband, acquired much the same legal character as the other property of a woman who contracted a marriage which brought her under the *manus mariti*.[1] It became

---

[9] Sohm, *Inst.*, § 96.   [10] *Post*, § 45.   [11] B. G., § 1230.
[12] *Ante*, §§ 3, 5.   [13] *Contra*, Spain, C. C., 1385; *cf. post*, § 42.
[1] *Ante*, § 25.

the property of the husband, and he disposed of it as freely as he did of his other property. The measures, referred to in the preceding section, which compelled the restitution of the dowry, did not affect the husband's power of disposition during the marriage. At the outset, they conferred upon the wife a right of action against the husband alone, and hence did not bind the dotal property in the hands of third parties.

The first limitation upon the husband's powers of disposition occurred in the legislation of Augustus. The *lex Julia de adulteriis*, prohibited the husband from alienating or encumbering certain dotal immovables.[2] The legislation of Justinian completed the development by extending the limitation to all dotal immovables[3] and by giving the wife other substantial remedies for the protection of her property rights.[4]

In strict form the husband still remains owner of the dotal effects, but it is a form that is deprived of all substance by positive exceptions and limitations. He retains the right of administration, but cannot alienate nor encumber any dotal immovable. For the further protection of the wife, and to guard her from the undue influence of the husband, such dispositions are considered invalid even if made with her consent.[5] Moreover, the wife, in addition to her personal claim against the husband, is given the right to sue as owner for the return of the dowry.[6] As such she can vindicate her immovables, but, with respect to movables, the right is limited to those which have not been alienated by the husband. Justinian's law, in fact, makes the wife the owner of the dowry, but binds her by the valid acts of her

[2] Bechmann, *Dotalrecht*, vol. ii, p. 445 *seq.*
[3] Cod., 5, 13, 15; Nov., 61.   [4] See *post*, § 34.
[5] Cod., 5, 13, 15; Nov., 61.
[6] Cod., 5, 12, 30; Bechmann, *Dotalrecht*, vol. ii, p. 468 *seq.*

marital administrator. The latter is in reality a mere usufructuary, but in accordance with the old theory, he is regarded, pending the wife's action for the restitution of her dowry, as the formal owner, whose activity is subjected ·to extensive limitations.

In the modern codes, the fictitious elements have largely disappeared. The general principle with which all of the systems start is that the husband is the administrator of the dowry, while the wife is the owner of the dotal effects.[7] The husband may and should exercise all of those acts of administration which an ordinary usufructuary has the right and obligation of undertaking. In accordance with the general principles governing usufruct, he becomes owner of that part of the dotal property which consists in money, negotiable instruments or other fungible things, while the wife has only a personal claim for the restoration of the value of these objects. The same result follows where movables are settled in dowry at a fixed estimate, unless it is expressly stipulated that the valuation is not intended to effect a sale of the property.[8] On the other hand, the valuation of dotal immovables will not be held to transfer title to the husband unless the sale is proven.[9]

To the extent that the husband does not become owner of the dowry, he does not possess the right to alienate or encumber the dotal effects. The codes differ respecting dispositions affecting such property. Some, following the

---

[7] Austria, B. G., §§ 1227, 1228; France, C. C., 1549, 1551 *seq.*, 1560, 1561; Italy, C. C., 1399, 1401 *seq.*, 1407; Spain, C. C., 1346, 1357; La., C. C., 2350.

[8] France. C. C., 1551; Italy, C. C., 1401; La., C. C., 2354. In Austria (B. G., § 1228), and Spain (C. C., 1346), the burden of proof is upon the husband and those claiming under him to show that the sale was made.

[9] Austria, B. G., § 1228; Spain, C. C., 1346; by express declaration: France, C. C., 1552; Italy, C. C., 1402; in Louisiana, they will not pass into the ownership of the husband even if an express agreement has been made, C. C., 2355.

Roman law, make a distinction between dotal movables and immovables. The mortgage or alienation of the latter is in general invalid, even if the wife gives her consent or joins in the act.[10] This rule has been influenced by the fear that the wife will suffer from the undue influence of the husband, as well as by the desire to keep the land intact for the benefit of the family. The provisions do not however constitute an absolute prohibition upon the alienation of dotal immovables. Certain exceptions are recognized on the ground of necessity or evident utility,[11] and also where such dispositions have been permitted by the contract of marriage.[12]

The Austrian and Spanish codes do not follow the Roman rule. In the former, there are no limitations upon the married woman's capacity of disposition, and, in accordance with the general principle,[13] it appears that she can freely alienate the dotal effects without the consent of her husband, subject always to his right of administration and usufruct during the marriage. In Spain, the wife, with the consent of her husband, may alienate or mortgage the dotal effects of which she has the ownership.[14]

The codes which distinguish between the disposition of

[10] France, C. C., 1554; Italy, C. C., 1405; La., C. C., 2357.

[11] They may be alienated: With wife's consent to endow children (France, C. C., 1555, 1556; La., C. C., 2358, 2359), or to make exchange for another immovable after official appraisement (France, C. C., 1559); with authorization of court for support of family, to release either party from prison, pay ante-nuptual debts of wife or party settling dower, make necessary repairs to dotal immovables, or affect necessary partition of property held in coparcenary (France, C. C., 1558; La., C. C., 2361, 2362). The Italian code makes a general exception where husband and wife consent and the court authorizes act upon ground of necessity or evident utility, C. C., 1405.

[12] France, C. C., 1557; Italy, C. C., 1404; La., but value must be reinvested in other immovables, C. C., 2360; *cf. ibid.*, 2355.

[13] *Ante*, §§ 2, 3.

[14] C. C., 1361. If wife is a minor, the intervention of party from whom dowry proceeds and the consent of the court are necessary.

dotal movables and immovables do not contain any special provisions respecting the alienation of the former. They can, accordingly, be disposed of by the wife, subject to the marital authorization which is required for such acts under these systems.[15]

§ 34. *Protection of the Dowry.*

Notwithstanding the limitations placed upon the husband's right of administration, the wife is generally accorded extensive privileges by way of further security for her dotal effects. An explanation of this attitude is to be found in the Roman law, which, while developing the substantial proprietary rights of the wife, continued the formal ownership of the husband. Moreover, the husband, at Roman law, had the power to alienate dotal movables. Accordingly the law of Justinian gave the wife a privileged legal mortgage which extended, independently of registration, over all of the husband's property.[1] Under the modern codes, the wife is unable to revoke any alienation until after the dissolution of the marriage.[2] And while it is expressly provided that dotal immovables shall be imprescriptible during the marriage,[3] this does not seem to be the rule respecting movables. Finally, it is considered necessary to protect the wife's interest in the estimated dowry, and in that which, by reason of its general character, passes into the ownership of the husband.

The legal mortgage of the wife for the protection of her dowry is recognized by the French and Italian codes. By virtue of this mortgage, the wife acquires a statutory lien

---

[15] *Ante,* § 3.

[1] Cod., 5, 13, 1; Inst., 4, 6, 29; Windscheid, *Pandekten*, vol. i, § 246, vol. ii, § 503.

[2] France, C. C., 1560; Italy, C. C., 1407; La., C. C., 2363.

[3] France, C. C., 1561; La., C. C., 2364, 3524.

over all the immovables possessed by the husband.[4] Such encumbrance obtains by operation of law and does not require public inscription for its validity. Provisions exist for restricting or barring such lien, but all such measures depend upon the express or implied consent of the wife, and judicial or other formalities must generally be observed.[5]

In Spain and Louisiana, the privilege of the wife is restricted to the right to have a mortgage recorded over the husband's property to secure her dowry.[6] In Austria, the wife is given no particular security by way of mortgage, but it is provided that the one who gives the dowry may demand suitable security, and, where the woman is under guardianship, the guardian can not dispense with such security except with consent of the court.[7]

All of the states recognize that, under certain conditions, the wife may demand that the husband shall be deprived of the administration of the dowry.

§ 35. *Separation of Property.*

The same conditions which lead to a separation of property under community systems will generally bring about the separation of the dowry from the property of which the husband has the administration.[1] In no case, however, do the modern codes recognize that separation of property is the

[4] France, C. C., 2121, 2135; Italy, C. C., 1969.

[5] France, C. C., 2140, 2144, 2193 *seq.;* Italy, C. C., 1969.

[6] Spain, C. C., 1349 *seq.;* where mortgage over husband's property is inadequate to cover value of stocks, bonds, etc., held in dowry, the titles of ownership must be publicly recorded, *ibid.*, 1355; La., C. C., 2376, 2377, 3252, 3254; the wife has also a privilege over ordinary creditors, in the husband's movables, *ibid.* 2376, 3191.

[7] B. G., § 1245.

[1] *Ante*, § 23.

legal result of the bankruptcy of the husband.[2]   The necessity for such result does not exist under this system as it
does under the system of marital administration and usufruct, or even of community.   The privileges which the wife
enjoys will enable her to protect the dowry and preserve its
fruits for the use of the family.

The separation of property may be demanded by the wife
and decreed by the court upon the same grounds as would
justify such action if community of property obtained between the married parties.[3]   In Austria, the separation may
be the result of mutual agreement, but the principle of the
invalidity of post-nuptial agreements forbids this in the other
countries.[4]

The dissolution of the marriage by death or divorce gives
ground for the separation of the dowry from the property of
the husband.   In some cases, as is generally true of community systems, the judicial separation of the parties will
produce the same result.[5]   In others, however, it confers
only a right to demand such separation.[6]

§ 36. *Restitution of the Dowry.*

The rule of Roman law, which was derived from the old
equitable *actio rei uxoriæ*,[1] was based upon the principle that

[2] In Austria, while bankruptcy dissolves the community of goods, it will not
bring about the separation of property where dowry exists.   It does not even
justify a demand for the restitution of the dowry, but only a claim to the security
for the future, and, under certain conditions, to the enjoyment of the dowry,
B. G., §§ 1260, 1261.

[3] France, C. C., 1563; Italy, C. C., 1448 *seq.;* Spain, C. C., 1365; La., C. C.,
2425 *seq.*

[4] *Ante*, § 3; Austria, B. G., § 1263.

[5] Spain, where husband is guilty party, C. C., 73; La., C. C., 155; *cf.* Austria,
B. G., § 1264.

[6] Italy, C. C., 1418; Austria, the innocent party may resist demand, B. G., §
1264.

[1] See, *ante*, § 32.

it would be unjust to require the husband to return immediately after separation the full amount of the dowry. The husband had the right to alienate movables, and where he had invested the capital resulting from such disposition, as well as from other dotal funds, it might entail considerable sacrifice if he were obliged to call in the same without delay. Hence he was allowed one year within which to make such restitution.[2] As he was not permitted to alienate immovables, these were to be returned at once.

The modern codes have been influenced by this rule. That part of the dowry of which the ownership remains in the wife, must be restored at once.[3] The remainder, including the value of fungible goods and of those objects that have been estimated and sold to the husband, need not be returned until the expiration of one year thereafter.[4] The husband is not held for the deterioration or destruction of dotal effects of which the wife retains the ownership, unless the damage has occurred through his fault.[5]

If the separation of goods is not accompanied by a dissolution of the marriage, the general rules governing the system of separate property come into operation.[6]

Following the Roman law,[7] the modern codes have particular regulations respecting the restitution of the dowry in case the separation of property is the result of divorce.

---

[2] Windscheid, *Pandekten*, vol. ii, § 502; the earlier rule gave him a longer period, *ibid.*, § 502, note 1.

[3] France, C. C., 1564; Italy, C. C., 1409; Spain, C. C., 1369; La., C. C., 2367, 2368.

[4] France, C. C., 1565; Italy, C. C., 1410; Spain, C. C., 1370; La., C. C., 2367, 2368.

[5] France, C. C., 1566, 1567; Italy, C. C., 1411, 1412; Spain, C. C., 1375.

[6] France, C. C., 1563, 1448 *seq.;* Italy, but the goods retain the dotal character and must be employed with authorization of the court, C. C., 1423, 1424; Spain, C. C., 1443; La., C. C., 2430, 2434, 2435; *cf.* Austria, B. G., §§ 1263, 1264, 1237.

[7] Sohm, *Inst.*, § 97.

The innocent party retains while the guilty party loses all of the advantages conferred by the other.[8] If the dissolution of the marriage results from the death of the wife, her dowry falls into her succession, which is entitled to the profits of the same from the day of the dissolution. If the death of the husband causes the dissolution, it is generally recognized that the wife may elect between the profits of her dowry during the year of mourning and alimentary support from the husband's succession for the same period.[9]

DIVISION IV.

SYSTEM OF SEPARATE PROPERTY.

§ 37. *Development of the System.*

The system of separate property interests between the husband and the wife obtains as a statutory or contractual system in the legislations of practically all of the important civilized states.[1] In the majority of the legislations it is defined as a distinct system, and where this is not the case, the definition of paraphernal or reserved property (*Vorbehaltsgut, biens réservés*), provides regulations which may readily lead to the establishment of such a régime. While the system is defined in most of the Continental codes, it is probable that it was not framed in any of them, with the exception of the civil code of Russia, the new code of Germany, and the draft code of Switzerland, with any expectation of its extensive application.[2] Primarily, it was intended to take

[8] France, C. C., 299, 300; Italy, C. C., 156; Spain, C. C., 73; La., C. C., 155; In Austria, the innocent party may demand the continuation or abrogation of the marriage agreements, B. G., § 1264.

[9] France, C. C., 1570; Italy, C. C., 1415; Spain, C. C., 1379; La., C. C., 2374.

[1] *Cf.*, table, *ante*, § 13.

[2] The Norwegian statute of June 29, 1888 (*An. étran.*, vol. 18, p. 762 *seq.*), shows distinct traces of an attempt to introduce separate property as the statutory system.

effect when the statutory system was set aside by operation of law or judicial decree. In England and the United States, on the contrary, it has become the regular statutory system.

The movement which has resulted in the substitution of the system of separate property for the English common law system of exclusive rights of the husband, covers a period of a little more than the latter half of the nineteenth century. It will be necessary to consider only the general character of the development in order to indicate the present conditions and tendencies of legislation in the field of matrimonial property relations.

The essential features of the English common law system have been indicated.[3] Whatever may have been the influences which affected and determined its development, it was a system based fundamentally upon the principle of the superiority of the man as the head of the family. It was quite natural that the recognition of the independent existence of the wife should come first from the customary rather than from the statutory sources of legislation. The English Court of Chancery was an organ for realizing social demands to which the conservatism of the legislators failed to respond.

As soon as personal property began to assume importance, the inequitable character of the common law system became manifest. At an early date the Court of Chancery recognized the wife's equity to a settlement out of her personal property which the husband had the legal right of reducing to his possession and ownership. This was a pure and simple act of legislation clothed under the forms of judicial fiction. It was not a principle that applied to all of the wife's personal property. The courts of common law would not enforce it with respect to personal property of the wife which came under their jurisdiction. In the beginning, it

Ante, § 25.

was only where the husband found it necessary to appeal to the Court of Chancery, in order to gain possession of his wife's personal property, *i. e.*, where the question involved came under the peculiar jurisdiction of such court, that the rule came into operation. The court said in effect: " You have the legal right to this property, but you are asking the assistance of a court whose essential function is the enforcement of equitable principles. It is a fundamental maxim that he who claims equity must do equity. It is unjust (unrighteous) and inequitable for you to take all of the property of the wife and thus leave her without any means of support, except such as you are willing to accord her. Hence, before we will give you possession of this property, you must settle a portion of the same upon your wife."

Beginning with the wife's equity to a settlement, the Court of Chancery gradually developed a system of separate property rights for the married woman, which it enforced, regardless of whether such rights were settled upon the wife by judicial decree, by act of the husband or by the intervention of a third party. It was sufficient if there was a clear intention to set aside the property for the separate use of the wife. In such an event, the Court of Chancery gave the property the character of a trust estate, and enforced the execution of the trust for the benefit of the wife. The estate assumed the character of the separate property, which is reserved under the system of marital administration and usufruct, for the use and profit of the wife.[4] The husband's common law rights were excluded, and the property was administered by the wife directly, or through the agency of a trustee, for her benefit.

This system gave efficient relief to those who were enabled to seek the assistance of the lawyers and the courts. But only the more wealthy and intelligent classes could

[4] *Ante*, § 26.

avail themselves of such a remedy. In those cases where
the rule was apt to work the severest hardships, as in the
case of women dependent upon the proceeds of their personal activity, the situation was quite similar to that which
may arise under community systems, where the sole protection of the wife is her right to demand separation of property.[5] The expense and complex character of the procedure precluded its application to such cases. Moreover, matrimonial property rights which cannot be enjoyed without
recourse to legal formalities and judicial procedure must always be limited in the extent of their use and enjoyment.
In the great majority of cases, parties on the eve of matri-
mony will scout the idea of the possible necessity of measures of security against each other. An equitable legal
definition of property rights is hence essential, not only for
the regulation of the relations in the normal marriage, but
also for the protection of those who come to grief as a result of misplaced confidence. It does not necessarily follow
that in the normal marriage the actual conditions of the administration and enjoyment of property will conform to the
statutory system. Under separate property systems the
wife will frequently entrust her property to her husband.[6]
The existence of legal rules, of which advantage may be
taken at any time, will, however, be a guarantee of the
preservation of equitable relations between the parties.

The operation of the English system, even after the establishment of the married woman's equitable separate estate,
revealed its radical defects. The wife, however extensive
the property which she has brought to the husband, has no
legal claim to be heard in the matter of its disposition or en-

[5] *Ante*, § 18.

[6] It has been declared that it is the custom in Russia for married parties to
hold and enjoy their goods in common (Lehr, *Droit Russe*, pp. 17, 41). Practically the same condition may be found in many American families.

joyment. However industrious and economical she may be, she can not claim the fruits of her activity, or the results of her savings. The husband, however extravagant, dissipated or worthless, has a legal right to all the acquisitions which proceed from the personal industry of the wife. This right, moreover, is not personal to the husband, but may be taken advantage of by his creditors.

It was under the influence of these conditions that the movement arose during the early part of the nineteenth century for a statutory definition of the married woman's separate property rights. This movement produced its first results in America, in acts according the wife certain rights of ndependent legal activity in case she has been deserted by her husband.[7] These were followed by statutes recognizing her separate rights in particular classes of property, such as in life insurance policies, deposits in savings banks, *etc.*,[8] and exempting such property from the husband's disposition and from liability for his debts.

About the middle of the century statutes appeared which accord the character of separate property to the entire fortune which the wife possessed at the time the marriage was contracted. From this period, the movement became general throughout the United States, one statute being soon supplanted by another affording greater privileges to the married woman. So earnest were the advocates of the reform that in many states, by bringing the question before the legislatures or constitutional conventions, they succeeded in having clauses inserted in the body of the organic law making it mandatory upon the legislative body to provide a system of separate property rights for married women or to

---

[7] *Cf.* proposal in France to give the wife in case of husband's misconduct, a right to control the proceeds of her labor, *ante*, § 18.

[8] *Cf.* recent similar acts in France and proposal in Belgium, *ante*, § 18, notes 9, 10; Norway, Stat., June 29, 1888, art. 20.

exempt their property from the husband's disposition or from liability for his debts.[9]

The legislation in the different states has been influenced by the earlier statutes, but while there is substantial agreement as to general purpose, the details are not worked out harmoniously. Some of the states have gone much further than others. In many instances the acts have been passed without due consideration of the consequences that would result, and it has frequently happened that the legislature, in according the wife free activity, has failed to repeal rules which conceded privileges to her on account of her incapacity of acting.[10] While the principle of separate property interests has been definitely accepted in practically all of the states which do not recognize community property, the formulation of the system has not been perfected. It has become a common saying that every legislative assembly amends the statutes respecting the property rights of married women. The later measures show a tendency to take the form of general statutes, defining systematically the matrimonial property relations.[11] It is quite significant that the recent amendments are often designed to correct, in the interests of third parties, the inconsistencies and lack of equity resulting from some of the earlier acts.

In Great Britain, the movement has been characterized by

---

[9] *Cf.* provisions in Constitutions of: Ala., art. x, § 6; Ark., art. ix, §§ 7, 8; Cal., art. xx, § 8; Fla., art. xi, §§ 1, 2; Geo., art. iii, § 11; Kans., art. xv, §6; Md. art. iii, § 43; Mich., art. xvi, § 5; Miss., § 94; Nevada, art. iv, § 31; N. C., art. x, §§ 6, 7; N. D., art. xvii, § 213; Oreg., art. xv, § 5; S. C., art. xvii, § 9; S. D., art. xxi, § 5; Texas, art. xvi, § 15: W. Va., art. vi, § 49.

[10] *Ante*, § 7.

[11] Several of such acts have been passed during the period in which the present study has been made. See Md., Laws, 1898, c. 457; N. Y. Laws, 1896, c. 272; Dist. of Col., Act, June 1, 1896, U. S. Stat. at Large, vol. 29, p. 193; *cf.* Penn., Act, June 8, 1893, Laws, p. 344; W. V., Acts, 1893, c. iii. In many states, the periodical revisions of the statutes have produced similar results.

greater conservatism. The legislations of the American states and the results of the same have been carefully investigated by parliamentary commissions. As a result, the statutes are more harmoniously framed and more consistent in their operation than the earlier American statutes. The first Married Women's Property Act was passed in 1870.[12] As was true of the first American statutes, it limited the character of separate property to certain objects,[13] and it was not until the Married Women's Property Act of 1882 [14] that all the property of the wife became impressed with this character. The above-named acts apply only to England and Ireland, but statutes, passed in 1877,[15] 1880 [16] and 1881,[17] introduce substantially the same system in Scotland, subject to modifications resulting from the peculiar development of matrimonial property relations in the latter country. The English-speaking colonies of Great Britain have generally followed the acts of the mother country with respect to the separate property rights of married women.

§ 38. *General Character of the Married Woman's Property.*

The normal condition under this system is for all the wife's property, of whatever nature, and whenever and however acquired, to be held in her own name, free from any claims on the part of her husband to any interest in the substance or in the fruits of the same. In considering the extent to which this condition has been realized in England and in most of the American states, it is necessary to keep in mind

[12] 33 and 34 Vict., c. 93.

[13] *Ibid.*, earnings of wife (§ 1), deposits in savings banks, public funds, stock in companies where no liability attaches to holding of the same (§§ 2-5), personal property, not exceeding £200, coming to wife during marriage by deed or succession (§ 7), rents and profits of real property falling to wife by intestate succession (§ 8), policies of life insurance (§ 10).

[14] 45 and 46 Vict., c. 75, § 2.   [15] Act, 40 and 41 Vict., c. 29.

[16] Act, 43 and 44 Vict., c. 26.   [17] Act, 44 and 45 Vict., c. 21.

the fact that the common law system prevails in so far as it has not been abrogated. A number of special privileges accorded the wife in particular kinds of property will not destroy the husband's general and residuary rights. To accomplish this, there must be a positive provision abrogating the common law system, or the wife must be granted general privileges sufficiently comprehensive to exclude the husband's common law rights.

The method pursued at first was to exempt certain kinds of property from the husband's usufruct or right of ownership and to reserve the same as the separate property of the wife.[1] This did not establish a system of separate property relations, but created merely a species of separate property for the wife, which was distinguished from her other property over which the husband exercised extensive rights. This separate property has been extended more or less rapidly in its scope until in some states it includes practically all of the property of the wife. Where this condition exists the legislation is generally simplified by the adoption of provisions giving the married woman the right to hold all of her property as a *femme sole*, or expressly abrogating all of the rights of the husband in his wife's property.

This last stage has been attained in Great Britain and in most of the American legislations, but the method of statutory definition is not the same. As previously indicated, the development of the system has not been completed in many instances, and the statutes in some cases remain in a chaotic condition. In eight of the American legislations positive provisions have been enacted expressly abrogating the common law effects of the marriage upon the property of the wife or of the married parties.[2] In addition, those

[1] *Ante*, § 37.

[2] For example of such provisions see *post*, Appendix, note A; Conn., G. S.,

legislations in which the community system has been introduced, have abrogated the common law rule so far as it obtained among them.[3]

In the great majority of the states either there is a provision in general terms that all of the property of the wife shall be her separate property or shall be held by her as if unmarried,[4] or there is a number of specific enactments followed by such a general clause,[5] or there is a series of general grants of property rights to the wife sufficiently comprehensive to produce the same result.[6]

Finally, there are nine states which, while providing in general or specific terms that all of the property of the married woman shall be her separate property, make an exception of objects donated by or acquired from the husband.[7] Similar limitations, which existed in other legisla-

---

1888, § 2796; Ky., Stat., 1894, § 2127; Me., R. S., 1883, c. 61, § 2; Miss., An. Code, 1892, § 2289; Mont., C. C., 1895, §§ 213, 220; N. D., R. C., 1895, §§ 2766, 2767; Oklah., R. S., 1893, § 2967; S. D., C. L., 1887, §§ 2588, 2600.

[3] *Ante*, § 17 (b).

[4] For examples of such provisions see *post*, Appendix, note B; N. C., Const., art. x, § 6; Ohio, R. S., 1891, § 3114; Oreg., An. Stat., 1887, § 2992, as amended by statute of Feb. 22, 1893 (Acts, p. 170); Penn., Statute of June 8, 1893, § 1 (Laws, p. 344); R. I., G. L., 1896, c. 194, § 1; Va., Code, 1887, § 2284; Hawaii, Laws, 1888, c. xi, § 1; Act, 45 and 46 Vict., c. 75, § 2.

[5] For example of such provisions see *post*, Appendix, note C; Ala., Code, 1896, §§ 2520–2523, 2530; Ark., Dig. Stat., 1894, §§ 4940, 4945; Ga., Code, § 2474; Md., Laws, 1898, c. 457, § 1; Mich., An. Stat., 1882, § 6295; Minn., G. S., 1894, § 5531: N. J., Act, Mch. 27, 1874, §§ 1, 3, 4, Rev., 1877, p. 636; N. Y., Laws, 1896, c. 272, §§ 20, 21; S. C., C. S. L., 1893, § 2164; Wis., An. Stat., 1889, §§ 2341, 2342, as amended by Laws, 1895, c. 86.

[6] For example of this class see *post*, Appendix, note D; Ill., An. Stat., 1885, c. 68, ¶¶ 7, 9; Ind., An. Stat., 1894, §§ 6962, 6975; Mo., R. S., 1899, § 4340; Utah, R. S., 1898, § 1198; Dist. of Col., Act, June 1, 1896, § 1, U. S. Stat. at Large, vol. 29, p. 193.

[7] For example of this class, see *post*, Appendix, note E; Col., gifts of money, jewelry and wearing apparel become her separate property, An. Stat., 1891, §§ 3007, 3012; Del., Laws, vol. 15, c. 165, § 1, R. C., 1893, p. 600; Kans., G. S., 1889, § 3752; Mass., gifts of wearing apparel and articles for personal use not

tions, have recently been repealed[8] and the general tendency is to permit such gifts to become the wife's separate property, subject, in some instances, to a proviso that the latter shall be liable for the debts of the husband existing at the time of the gift, and in all cases to the rules against gifts in fraud of creditors.[9]

Of a similar character are the rules governing the beneficial interest of the wife in policies of insurance upon the life of her husband. It has been indicated previously that such provisions arose before the married woman was accorded a general right of holding her property for her separate use. The acts generally provided that where a married woman was the beneficiary in an insurance policy, whether the latter had been contracted by the husband, the wife or a third party, the proceeds of the same should be for her sole use and benefit. The effect was to create a trust in favor of the wife. With the development of the investment feature in life insurance, the danger arose that such policies in favor of the wife might be utilized for the purpose of defrauding the husband's creditors of the means for satisfying their claims. Hence, in some states, qualifications exist limiting the amount of the annual premium that may be paid out of the property of the husband, and providing that any excess in the premium or in the insurance effected thereby, shall be the husband's property or shall be liable for his debts.[10]   In

exceeding $2,000 in value, become her separate property, P. S., 1882, c. 147, §§ 1–3, as amended by Acts, 1884, c. 132 and Acts, 1889, c. 204; Neb., C. S., 1891, § 1411; N. H., P. S., 1891, c. 176, § 1; Vt., Stat, 1894, § 2647; W. Va., Code, 1891, c. 66, §§ 2, 3, as amended by Acts, 1893, c. iii; Wy., R. S., 188-. § 1558. *Cf. ante*, § 5.

[8] Wis., An. Stat., 1889, § 2342, Laws, 1895, c. 86; Dist. of Col., R. S., 1873–74, §727, Act, June 1, 1896, § 1, U. S. Stat. at Large, vol. 29, p. 193.

[9] *Ante*, § 5.

[10] The maximum premiums are as follows: Ala., $500, Code, 1896, § 2535; Mich., $300, An. Stat., 1882, § 6300; N. Y., $500, Laws, 1896, c. 272, §22; Ohio,

other states, there is either an express provision that premiums paid in fraud of creditors shall inure to their benefit, or the general rule against such transactions will qualify the wife's interest in such property to the extent that the frauds can be presumed or proven.[11]

Of the American states in which individual matrimonial property systems exist, Florida and Tennessee are the only ones which fail to recognize that the normal condition of the wife's fortune is that obtaining under the system of separate property. In the former state, the constitution as well as the statutes, declare that the property of the wife shall be her separate property and not liable for the debts of her husband.[12] Nevertheless the husband has the administration of such property and the wife is forbidden to sue him for the profits and proceeds of the same. Thus the property of the married woman is dotal rather than separate, and the system is that of marital administration and usufruct. The statutes, however, recognize separate property in the strict sense as existing in the earnings of the wife,[13] her deposits in banks[14] and stock held by her in building and loan associations.[15] Moreover, the court, if satisfied as to her qualifications, may, after certain formalities have been observed, grant the wife a license to become a free dealer, in which case all of her property becomes separate and she controls the same as if unmarried.[16]

In Tennessee it is recognized that separate property of a married woman may be established by donation, testament-

---

$150, R. S., 1891, § 3628; Vt., $300, even if insurance is effected by wife, Stat., 1894, §§ 2653-2657; W. Va., $150, Code, 1891, c. 66, § 5, as amended by Acts, 1893, c. iii; Hawaii, $500, Act of 1868, C. L., 1884, p. 429; *cf.* Wis., An. Stat., 1888, §2347, as amended by Laws, 1891, c. 376.

[11] *Ante*, § 5.   [12] Fla., Const., art. xi, §1, R. S., 1892, § 2070.

[13] Fla., R. S., 1892, § 2075.   [14] *Ibid.*, §2199.

[15] *Ibid.*, §2208.   [16] *Ibid.*, §§ 1505-1508.

ary or *inter vivos*, as well as by grant.[17]   There is also a
statutory separatee state in insurance policies,[18] deposits in
banks [19] and stock in building and loan associations.[20]   Moreover, if the husband has deserted his wife or is insane, the
latter will acquire property for her separate account.[21]
Under ordinary conditions, however, where no positive stip-
ulations have been made, the woman's property, as a result
of the marriage, becomes subjected to the husband's common law rights, which have been modified somewhat in the
interests of the wife.[22]

In Russia, it is the statutory rule that the marriage does
not affect the property of either party.   That which the wife
possesses at the time of the marriage or afterwards acquires
in any legal manner, is her separate property.[23]

In those codes in which the system of separate property is
a contractual or extraordinary statutory system, it is the
regular rule that where such system obtains, all of the wife's
fortune shall become her separate property.

§39. *Products of the Personal Industry of the Married
Woman.*

Where the perfect system of separate property obtains,
the married woman has the same rights over the proceeds
of her personal industry as those which she possesses with
respect to her other property.   This is recognized in all of
the systems of Continental Europe.   The codes do not contain express provisions with reference to such property.
These are unnecessary under this system, as well as under
the system of dowry.   The general principle in both systems is that the economic interests of the woman are un-

[17] *Code*, 1884, § 3343.   [18] *Ibid.*, §§ 3335, 3336.
[19] *Ibid.*, § 1729.   [20] *Ibid.*, § 1757.
[21] *Ibid.*, § 3344, *seq.*   [22] *Ibid.*, §§ 3338–3341.
[23] Leuthold, *R. R.*, p. 59; Lehr, *Droit Russe*, p. 42.

affected by the marriage, and hence, unless there is a positive exception, she possesses the right to receive and to hold her earnings as her separate property.[1] The question of her personal right to engage in particular undertakings depends upon different considerations which have been previously considered.[2] While the married woman may be limited in her right to engage in certain activities, she can not be deprived of the proceeds which result from an enterprise which she is permitted to undertake.

The English common law principle that the husband is entitled to all that which his wife gains by her personal activity, probably had its chief basis in the fact that he had an absolute right to her personal property. It was also connected with his right to the services of the wife. When the courts came to construe the married women's acts, they followed the strict rule of interpretation of statutes in derogation of the common law, and held that the provisions that the property of the wife should be held to her separate use, did not deprive the husband of his right to the latter's earnings. It was argued that his right to his wife's services was not affected by the property acts, and hence he continued to possess his right to the proceeds of her personal activity.

Where the statutes have expressly abrogated the common law effects of the marriage upon the property of the wife, or have declared that all of the property of the married woman, however acquired, shall be her separate estate,[3] it would appear that the wife's earnings would become her separate property. Most of the states have placed the matter be-

[1] Bridel, *Femme mariée*, p. 4; Guntzberger, pp. 92, 96, 97; Pascaud, "Le Droit de la Femme mariée aux Produits de son Travail," *Rev. pol. et parle*, vol. ix, pp. 570, 571.

[2] *Ante*, § 6.

[3] See *ante*, § 38, and *cf.* statutory provisions, *post*, Appendix.

yond question by positive statutory provisions giving the
wife the sole right to the products of her personal industry.
A qualification generally exists however that she shall not be
entitled to compensation for services rendered to her husband or family.[4] In a few of the states, the provision is
that the wife's earnings shall not be liable for the debts
of her husband.[5]

§ 40. *Dower and Curtesy.*

The widow's dower and the husband's curtesy are peculiar
creations of the English common law. Representing at
once elements of matrimonial property relationships and
rights of succession, they indicate the intimate connection
existing between these legal relations.[1] These institutions
continued for many centuries as essential features of the
legal property relations of husband and wife. During the
nineteenth century, however, they have suffered considerable modification in some legislations, and in others they
have been entirely abrogated.[2]

[4] Ala., Code, 1896, § 2531; Ark., Dig. Stat., 1894, § 4945; Conn., G. S., 1888
§§ 2790, 2796; Del., R. C., 1893, c. 76, § 3; Fla., R. S., 1892, § 2075; Ill., An.
Stat., 1885, c. 68, ¶ 8; Ind., An. St., 1894, § 6975; Iowa, Code, 1897, § 3162;
Me., R. S., 1883, c. 61, § 3; Mass., P. S., 1882, c. 147, § 4; Minn., G. S., 1894,
§ 5531; Miss., An. Code, 1882, § 2293; Mo., R. S., 1899, § 4340; Mont., C. C.,
1895, § 225; Neb., C. S., 1891, § 1414; N. H., P. S., 1891, c. 176, § 1; N. J.,
Act, Mch. 27, 1874, § 4, Rev., 1877, p. 637; N. Y., Laws, 1896, c. 272, § 21;
Oreg., An. St., 1887, § 2993; S. C., C. S. L., 1893, § 2165; Utah, R. S., 1898,
§ 1201; Vt., Stat., 1894, § 2647, Acts, 1888, p. 98; Va., Code, 1887, § 2287;
W. Va., Code, 1891, c. 66, § 12 as enacted by Acts, 1893, c. iii; Wis., An. St.,
1889, § 2343; Wy., R. S., 1887, § 1562; Dist. of Col., Act, June 1, 1896, § 3,
U. S. Stat. at Large, vol. 29, p. 193; Hawaii, Laws, 1888, c. xi, § 3; England
and Ireland, Act, 33 and 34 Vict., c. 93, § 1, Act, 45 and 46 Vict., c. 75, § 2;
Scotland, Act, 40 and 41 Vict., c. 29, § 3.

[5] N. D., R. C., 1895, § 2770; Oklah., R. S., 1893, § 2972; R. I., G. S., 1896,
c. 255, § 5; S. D., C. L., 1887, § 2594. *Cf.* rule in American community systems,
ante, § 18.

[1] *Cf. post,* § 45.

[2] See rhetorical soliloquy of an old lawyer occasioned by the abolition of dower
and curtesy in Mississippi in 1880, *post,* Appendix, note F.

With the development of real estate transactions, it was inevitable that such provisions should prove inconvenient and that hardships, and even injustice, should frequently occur. It was natural that a demand should be made for a modification of the rules governing the wife's interest in the husband's lands. Thus, in England, in 1833, it was enacted that "no widow shall be entitled to dower out of any land which shall have been absolutely disposed of by her husband in his lifetime, or by his will."[3] Moreover, a simple declaration in the husband's will is sufficient to bar the widow from any dower in his lands of which he dies intestate.[4] The widow's dower is also made secondary to all interests or charges created by any disposition of the husband to which his land is subject, including simple debts, as well as formal encumbrances.[5] These profound breaches in the old system were part of a general movement[6] to relieve the alienation of land of the obstacles and cumbersome procedure of the common law.[7] That it was not primarily intended to deprive the wife of any interest in her husband's lands is indicated by the fact that the act extended her dower right to trust estates and mere rights of entry.[8]

In the United States the legislation has been influenced not only by the same considerations, but also by the effects of the married women's acts. The latter, by taking away the husband's interest in his wife's property, removed a condition which many believed was the justification for the exist-

[3] Act, 3 and 4 Wm. IV., c. 105, § 4.

[4] *Ibid.*, § 7.   [5] *Ibid.*, § 5.

[6] The husband's curtesy was not affected by the above act, but marriage settlements in England have to a great extent caused its disappearance. Schouler, *H. & W.*, § 423.

[7] An act, of the same session, which abolished fines and recoveries, provided a method for alienating the lands of a married woman. Act, 3 and 4 Wm. IV., c. 74, § 77 *seq.; cf. post*, § 42.

[8] Act, 3 and 4 Wm. IV., c. 105, §§ 2, 3.

ence of dower. Here, also, the states have failed to follow
a uniform policy.   Some have been more strongly influenced
by the one motive than by the other, and different methods have been adopted for realizing the desired end.   Thus,
some legislations have entirely abolished dower and curtesy,[9]
while in others the dower has been continued but made to
apply equally to the husband and to the wife.[10] Some states
have abolished dower and curtesy but have instituted in
their stead other estates generally more extensive in scope.[11]
In a few cases the interest has been limited to a legal or intestate portion in the succession, by being confined to the
real property of which the party died seized.[12]

[9] Cal., C. C., § 173; Col., An. St., 1891, § 1524; Conn., G. S., 1888, § 2796;
Idaho, R. S., 1887, § 2506; Miss., An. Code, 1892, § 2291; Nev., G. S., 1885,
§ 505; N. D., R. C., 1895, §§ 2770, 3743; Oklah., R. S., 1893, § 6262, probably
inoperative so far as dower is concerned, *cf.* Act, Mch. 3, 1887, § 18, U. S. Stat.
at Large, vol. 24, pp. 638, 639; S. D., C. L., 1887, §§ 2594, 3402; Wash., G. S.,
1891, § 1405; Wy., R. S., 1887, § 2221. Neither dower nor curtesy obtains in
Louisiana or Texas.

[10] Ill., An. St., 1885, c. 41, ¶ 1; Ky., Stat., 1894, § 2132; Me., but husband's
interest is dependent upon solvency of wife's estate, R. S., 1883, c. 103, §§ 1, 14;
Md., Laws, 1898, c. 457, §§ 6, 7; Ohio, R. S., 1891, § 4188; Oreg., wife's dower
is increased to life interest in one-half of husband's lands and husband's curtesy
attaches even if marriage is without issue, Statute, Feb. 22, 1883, Acts, p. 194,
An. St., 1887, § 2983.

[11] In all real property, of which decedent was seized during coverture, to the
conveyance of which the survivor has not consented: ⅓ in fee simple: Ind., as
against creditors, wife takes only ¼ or ¹/₅ if the property exceeds $10,000 or
$20,000 respectively (An. St., 1894, §§ 2639, 2640, 2652, 6961), while husband's
interest is subject to wife's ante-nuptial debts (*Ibid.*, §2642); Iowa, Code, 1897,
§§ 3366, 3376; Minn., subject to debts which are not satisfied out of personal
estate, G. S., 1894, § 4471; Neb., G. S., 1891, § 1124; ½ in fee simple: Kans.,
except in that sold at public auction or necessary for the payment of debts, G. S.,
1889, §§ 2599, 2619.

[12] Dower: Geo., Code, 1895, § 4687; N. H., P. S., 1891, c. 195, § 3; Tenn.,
Code, 1884, §§ 3244 *seq.*, 3251; Vermont, ⅓ in fee simple, Pub. Acts, 1896, no.
44, §§ 1, 2. Curtesy: Ark., Dig. Stat., 1894, § 4945, Neely v. Lancaster, 47, Ark.
175; Vt., ⅓ in fee simple, but limited to property of which both husband and
wife are seized in her right, Pub. Acts, 1896, no. 44, § 15; Wis., does not attach
if issue of wife by former marriage exists, An. St., 1889, § 2180.

In a number of states the statutory provisions recognize the widow's dower alone.[13] The husband's common law curtesy exists in these states,[14] except where it has been expressly or impliedly abrogated or modified.[15] There are, finally, a few states that define dower and curtesy substantially as they existed at common law.[16]

Where the common law dower or curtesy obtains, or where the interest of one party extends to all of the lands of which the other was seized during the marriage, every conveyance or disposition of the property will be subject to such interest unless the party entitled participates in the act or his interest is barred by the acceptance of a pecuniary

[13] Ala., subject to reduction in proportion to wife's separate estate, Code, 1896, §§ 1500, 1508; Ark., Dig. Stat., 1894, §2520, see preceding note for rule as to curtesy; Fla., R. S., 1892, §1830; Mont., C. C., 1895, § 228; N. Y., Laws, 1896, c. 547, § 170 *seq.*; S. C., C. S. L., 1893, § 1900 *seq.*; Utah, dower and curtesy are abolished, but wife is given substantially the same, except that she takes ⅓ in fee simple, R. S., 1898, §§ 2826, 2832; Wis., An. St., 1889, § 2159, see preceding note for rule respecting curtesy; Dist. of Col., Act, June 1, 1896, § 10, U. S. Stat. at Large, vol. 29, p. 193. By the Edmunds-Tucker Act of Mch. 3, 1887 (§ 18, U. S. Stat. at Large, vol. 24, pp. 638, 639), the widow's common law dower was established for the territories of the United States. Thus, it would appear that the widow can claim this right independent of the acts of the territorial legislature.

[14] It is recognized by positive provisions in some states that have modified the widow's dower. *Cf.* N. H., P. S., 1891, c. 195, § 9; Penn., even if marriage is without issue, Dig., 1883, p. 930, §4; Tenn., Code, 1884, § 3351.

[15] It has been abrogated in Ariz., R. S., 1887, § 225; Geo., Code, 1895, § 3094; Mont., C. C., 1895, § 257; S. C., C. S. L., 1893, §2169; *cf.* Me., R. S., 1883, c. 61, § 2.

[16] Del., R. C., 1893, c. 87, § 1, c. 85, § 1, c. 76, Act, Apl. 9, 1873, § 5; Mass., P. S., 1882, c. 124, §§ 1, 2, if no issue, the husband has life estate in one-half of wife's lands, Acts, 1885, c. 255, § 2; Mich., An. St., 1882, §§ 5733, 5783, it appears that husband's curtesy will not attach to wife's separate estate (*ibid.*, §6295), and in no case if wife has issue by a former marriage (*ibid.*, § 5770); Mo., R. S., 1899, §§ 2933, 111; N. J., Rev., 1877, p. 298, § 6, p. 320, § 1; R. I., G. L., 1896, c. 194, § 9, c. 203, § 12, c. 264, § 1; N. C., Code, 1883, §§ 2102, 2103, 1838; Va., Code, 1887, §§ 2267, 2286; W. Va., Code, 1891, c. 65, § 1. Husband has curtesy even if marriage is without issue, *ibid*, § 15.

provision expressly or impliedly made in lieu thereof. Where the survivor is granted an intestate right of succession or a legal portion in real property, the acceptance of such interest will generally bar any claim to dower or curtesy.[17]

§ 41. *Homestead.*

In American states, the homestead and exemption laws have created for married persons common interests in their respective properties. The primary purpose of such statutes has been to provide for the support of the family in the event of the insolvency of its head. They provide for the exemption of the homestead from execution, the maximum amount of land and the value of the same varying in the different states. Personal property of a certain character and value is also generally exempted from execution for the debts of the owner. In order to secure such property for the future needs of the family and to prevent the husband from sacrificing the same, it is very generally provided that no disposition of the homestead or mortgage of the exempt personal property shall be valid without the joinder of the wife in the deed.

As an interesting result of the married women's acts, the wife, in many states, is permitted to select a homestead and to hold certain personal property exempt from execution by her creditors. In some states this results from express statutory provisions,[1] while in others the enactment that

---

[17] *Cf. post*, §§ 46, 47. The conduct of the party may also lead to barring of such interest.

[1] Geo., if wife with minor child lives separate from husband, Code, 1895, § 2842; Ind. An. St., 1894, § 6969; Iowa, Code, 1897, § 2978; Md., Laws, 1898, c. 355; Mich., An. St., 1882, §§ 7728, 7729; Miss., An. Code, 1892, §§ 1970, 1984; Mo. R. S., 1899, § 4335; Mont. C. C., 1895, § 1671; N. H., P. S., 1891, c. 138, § 1; N. Y., C. C. P., §§ 1392, 1397; Ohio, R. S., 1891, § 5435; Oklah., Laws, 1897, c. 8, § 5; Oreg., Laws, 1893, p. 93; N. D., R. C., 1895, §§ 3606,

owners or householders are entitled to the privilege would seem to include married women.[2] In the later statutes, it is generally provided that husband and wife shall not both be permitted to claim such exemptions.

The provisions limiting the disposition of the homestead do not apply eqnally to the husband and the wife. Most of the acts were framed in the expectation that the exempted property would be selected from that belonging to the husband. The provision that no disposition of the homestead shall be valid without the consent of the wife does not limit her disposition of the same where it has been selected from her own property. There is, however, a distinct tendency to require the consent of each married party to every disposition affecting the title of a homestead claimed by or selected out of the property of the other. The homestead thus becomes a species of common property and the rules of succession emphasize this character.[3]

§ 42. *Administration of the Wife's Property.*

The general rule, recognized in all of the legislations, is that the wife alone is competent and qualified to perform all acts of simple administration over her separate property. In

3621; S. C., C. S. L., 1893, § 2132; S. D., C. L., 1887, §2456, *seq.*; Utah, R. S., 1898, §§ 1149, 1152, 1154; Wash., Laws, 1895, c. 64; W. Va., Code, 1891, c. 41, §§ 23, 30; Dist. of Col., Act, June 1, 1896, § 5, U. S. Stat. at Large, vol. 29, p. 193; *cf.* La. Const., 1898, art. 244. In following, husband must join wife in making claim to homestead out of her separate property: Ariz., R. S., 1887, § 2074; Cal. C. C., §§ 1238, 1239; Idaho, R. S., 1887, §§ 3036, 3037; Nev., G. S., 1885, § 539.

[2] Ala., Const., art. x, § 2; Conn. G. S., 1888, §2783; Ill., An. St., 1885, c. 52, ¶ 1; Kans., Const., art. 15, § 9; Ky., Stat., 1894, § 1702; Me., R. S., 1883, c. 81, §§ 63-66; Mass., P. S., 1882, c. 123, § 1; Minn., G. S., 1894, § 5521; N. J., Rev., 1877, p. 1055, §1; N. C., Const., art. x, § 2; Vt. Stat., 1894, § 2179; Va., Code, 1887, §§ 3630, 3650-3652; Wis., An. St., 1889, § 2983; Wy., R. S., 1887, § 2780.

[3] *Cf. post,* § 48.

this respect she acts as a *femme sole*.[1]   The husband does
not have a right to such administration.   It is, nevertheless,
recognized by some of the statutes that the marriage establishes such an intimate relation between the parties as to
justify the presumption that the wife has entrusted the husband with the administration of her goods,[2] and where, as a
matter of fact, she permits her husband to exercise such
functions over her property, she will not be able, in the absence of an express agreement, to hold him accountable for
the expenditure which he has made of the fruits and profits
resulting from his administration.[3]

With respect to administration in the broader sense, including the right of encumbering and alienating the separate
property, there is not such general agreement.   As an aid in
determining this question it will be well to refer to the general attitude of the legislations respecting the contractual
capacity of married women.[4]   In those that accept the principle that the wife has the same general capacity to make
contracts as is possessed by the unmarried woman, she will
have the power to dispose of her separate property unless
special provisions to the contrary exist.   On the other hand,
according to the legislations that regard the marriage as
qualifying the general contractual capacity of the woman,
the wife will have the right to make only such dispositions of
her property as are within the scope of her granted powers.

---

[1] *Contra* in Texas, where the husband has the sole management of the property
and wife has only a limited right of administration, R. S., 1895, §§ 2967, 2970,
2971; *cf.* rule in Florida and Tennessee, *ante*, § 38, note 13, *seq.*

[2] Austria, B. G., § 1238; only as regards paraphernalia under system of dowry:
France, C. C., 1578; Italy, C. C., 1429; La. C. C., 2385.   *Contra*, Spain, C. C.,
1383, 1384; Basle, Stat., Mch. 10, 1884, art. 30.

[3] Austria, B. G., § 1293; Germany, B. G., § 1430; France, C. C., 1539, 1578;
Italy, C. C., 1429; La., C. C., 2386; Switz., *Vorentwurf*, 271.

[4] See *ante*, § 3.

On this question, the legislations divide themselves into three classes:

I. Where the wife has the general right of disposition over all her separate property. This is subject, of course, to particular provisions governing dispositions between husband and wife, contracts of surety, donations, *etc.*[5]

II. Where the married woman is limited in the disposition of her immovables.

III. Where the wife is restricted in the disposition of her property in general.

The first class includes those states that have continued the rule of Roman law, as well as a majority of the newer legislations. Most of them recognize that the general contractual capacity of the woman is unaffected by the marriage, and hence particular provisions are unnecessary.[6]

Most of the American states that are not included in the first group, constitute the second division, which limits the married woman in dispositions affecting her real property. The peculiar sanctity which feudal ideas conferred upon land and the desire to preserve such property for the family have influenced these restrictions. It is necessary to note that the existing limitations were primarily designed to facilitate rather than to restrict the conveyance of the wife's real property. At common law such property was regarded as inalienable whether the husband acted alone or jointly

---

[5] *Cf. ante,* §§ 3–5.

[6] The following are included (*cf.* references, *ante,* §§ 2, 3): Austria, Germany, Prussia (but consent of husband is necessary for contracts of sale or pledge of jewelry or articles of adornment, A. L. R., ii, 1, § 223), Saxony, Russia, Norway, Basle, Glaris, Lucerne, Zürich, Draft Code of Switzerland, England, Alabama, Arizona, Arkansas, California, Colorado, Connecticut, Delaware, Georgia, Illinois, Iowa, Kansas, Maine, Maryland, Massachusetts, Michigan, Mississippi, Montana, Nebraska, New York, North Dakota, Ohio, Oklahoma, Oregon, Rhode Island, South Dakota, Tennessee, Utah, Virginia, Washington, Wisconsin, Wyoming, District of Columbia, Hawaii.

with his wife. The procedure which was devised to evade such restriction, was cumbersome in its operation and was abrogated as a result of the general movement to abolish antiquated obstacles to the transfer of land.[7] The joinder of the husband and wife in the deed of conveyance, executed with more or less formality, came to be sufficient to pass the title of the wife's real property.[8] With the barring of the husband's interest in the wife's lands and the conferring of general contractual capacity upon the married woman, the tendency has appeared to remove the remaining restrictions.[9]

The general rule that the joinder of the husband and wife is necessary to a valid conveyance of her real property still obtains in a number of states.[10] The provision intended to protect the wife from undue influence by requiring her separate examination respecting the voluntary character of the act, is also retained in a few statutes.[11] The protection of

---

[7] *Cf. ante*, § 40.

[8] Act, 3 & 4 Wm. IV., c. 74, § 77 *seq.* Custom and statutes in American states introduced similar rules.

[9] Recent abrogations have been made in: Ala., *cf.* Code, 1886, § 2346, with Code, 1896, § 2526; Ark., the courts having decided that wife could not make executory contracts to convey land (Christman *v.* Partee, 38 Ark., 31; Walters *v.* Wagley, 53 Ark., 509), an act of 1895 gave her this power (Laws, p. 58); Cal., Stat. & Amend., 1891, p. 137, *ibid.*, 1895, p. 53; Md. *cf.* P. G. L., 1888, art. 45, § 2, with Laws, 1898, c. 457, §§ 4, 5.

[10] Fla., R. S., 1892, § 1956; Idaho, R. S., 1887, § 2922; Ind., An. Stat., 1894, § 6961; Ky., Stat., 1894, § 2128; Minn., G. S., 1894, §§ 5530, 5532; Mo., R. S., 1899, § 901; Nev., G. S., 1885, §§ 2570, 2588 *seq.*; N. H., P. S., 1891, c. 176, § 3; N. J., Act, Mch. 27, 1874, § 14, Rev., 1877, p. 637; N. M., C. L., 1897, § 1510; N. C., Code, 1883, §§ 1826, 1834; Penn., Act, June 8, 1893, §§ 1, 2, Laws, p. 344; Tenn., Code, 1884, §§ 3338–3340; Vt., Stat., 1884, § 2646; W. Va., Acts, 1893, c. iii, §§ 2, 3; *cf.* Texas, R. S., 1895, art. 635.

[11] Idaho, R. S., 1887, §§ 2922, 2956, 2960; Ky., Stat., 1894, § 507; N. C., Code, 1883, §§ 1834, 1246, 1256; Tenn., Code, 1884, § 3340; *cf.* La., C. C., 127, 128; Texas, R. S., 1895, arts. 635, 4618, 4621.

the husband's curtesy appears to be the chief reason for the
retention of the restriction in the other legislations.[12]

The third class includes legislations in which the system
of separate property is regarded as unusual, and in which
the married woman is generally restricted in her contractual
capacity. The chief representatives of this class are the French
Civil Code and those Codes that have been most strongly influenced by it. The provisions of the codes are somewhat
obscure and, in some instances, conflict with each other.
The starting point is the general provision that the wife, even
if living under the separate property system, can not acquire
or alienate property without the consent or joinder of her
husband.[13] This principle is adhered to so far as separate
property (paraphernalia) under the system of dowry is concerned. The wife has the management, but is restricted in
dispositions over the substance of the goods.[14]

A distinction is made respecting the system of separate
property, according as it is the result of a judicial separation or of a marriage contract. In the former case, it is expressly provided that the wife may dispose of her movables
and alienate the same.[15] In the case of contractual separate

[12] Wherever the common law right of curtesy exists, any disposition by the
wife, even if she possesses the general right of alienating her real property, will
be subject to the conditional estate of the husband, *cf. ante*, § 40.

[13] France, C. C., 217; La., C. C., 122; *cf.* Finland, Stat., Apl. 15, 1889, c. ii, art.
6. In Spain the limitation is general, but does not contain the specific reference
to the system of separate property, C. C., 61. The Italian code does not contain
the specific reference to the system of separate property, and is limited to alienation or mortgage of immovables, contracting of loans and assignment or recovery
of stocks, C. C., 134.

[14] France, C. C., 1576; Spain, C. C., 1344, 1387; La., C. C., 2384, 2390; *cf.*
Italy, C. C., 1427, 134.

[15] France, C. C., 1449; La., C. C., 2435; in Spain the wife has the same power
over her property as the husband when he administers her goods, but she cannot
alienate or engage her immovables without judicial anthorization, C. C., 1442,
1444; in Finland she may dispose of her property as a widow, Stat., Apl. 15, 1889,
c. v, art. 15.

property, the codes are silent respecting the alienability of movables, but contain provisions expressly prohibiting the alienation of immovables without proper authorization.[16] It has been argued that the fact that emphasis is placed upon the prohibition of the alienation of immovables must be taken as evidence that the alienation of movables is permitted, as under the system of judicial separate property. This seems to be the prevailing view[17] despite the positive statements of the general provision limiting the powers of the wife.[18]

§ 43. *Support of the Family.*

The equitable character of a matrimonial property system will be affected by the provision that is made for the liquidation of the charges of the conjugal society. In all of the systems previously considered, the chief justification for the privileges which the husband possesses in his wife's property is to be found in the fact that he supports the expenses of the family household. Under the system of separate property, the husband is not entitled to any gain from the property of the wife. Moreover, the increasing extent to which women are engaging in industrial and other pursuits, tends to decrease the economic value of the personal services which the wife renders the family. The interests of third parties are likewise concerned. Where the husband becomes incapable of sustaining the matrimonial charges, shall creditors who have furnished supplies for the family suffer losses, while the wife, who has contributed to the expenses

[16] France, C. C., 1538; La., C. C., 2397; in Spain, it would appear that the same rule obtains as where the system is the result of judicial decrees, *cf.* C. C., 1432, 1442, 1444.

[17] *Cf.* Guntzberger, pp. 105, 98, 99. Respecting the tendency to apply the same rule to movables of the paraphernalia, see *ibid.*, p. 93 *seq.*

[18] *Cf. ante*, note 13.

for which the debts have been incurred, possesses ample means for liquidating such obligations?

Many states recognize that equitable considerations demand that the wife, who is able, shall assist in bearing the burden of the family expenses. In some cases the principle of joint liability has been adopted, the expenses of the family being chargeable upon the property of the husband and wife or of either of them.[1] Other legislations make the wife only secondarily liable, postponing execution upon her property until the failure of the husband's property to satisfy the debts, or granting her a right of indemnification against her husband.[2]

The legislations of Continental Europe generally require the wife to make a contribution out of the income of her property and the proceeds of her labor. In some cases it is provided that the contributions shall be suitable, or in proportion to the resources of the two parties,[3] while in other instances, a definite proportion of her income is required.[4] Particular provisions exist for the case where the system of

[1] Col., Act, Apl. 6, 1891, Laws, p. 238; Ill. An. St., 1885, c. 68, ¶ 15; Iowa, Code, 1897, § 3165; Mo., wife's separate personal property is liable for debts for necessaries, R. S., 1899, § 4340; N. M., if for necessaries, C. L., 1897, § 1511; Oreg., An. St., 1887, § 2874; Utah R. S., 1898, § 1206; Wash., G. S., 1891, § 1414.

[2] Ariz., where wife contracts debts upon her husband's credit, R. S., 1887, §§ 2107, 2108; Conn., G. S., 1888, § 2797; Neb., C. S., 1891, § 1411; Penn., Dig., 1883, p. 1151, § 15; *cf.* Mont., C. C., 1895, § 212; for maintenance of children: England, Act, 33 & 34 Vict., c. 93, § 14; Act, 45 & 46 Vict., c. 75, § 21; Leuthold, *R. R.*, p. 68; *cf.* Idado, R. S., 1887, § 5859; Nev. G. S., 1885, § 537.

[3] Germany, B. G., § 1427; Italy, C. C., 1426, 138; Spain, C. C., 1434; Switz., *Vorentwurf*, 274.

[4] France, ⅓, C. C., 1537, 1575; La., ½, C. C., 2388, 2395; Basle, ½ and if husband is incapable, all, Stat., Mch. 19, 1884, art. 31; in Spain the profits of paraphernal property are employed in defraying the matrimonial charges and the substance may be taken in case the dowry and the husband's property are insufficient, C. C., 1385.

separate property is the result of judicial decree. The contribution, in such event, must generally be in proportion to the resources of the two parties, and may affect the substance of the wife's property as well as her income.[5]

The married woman may indirectly be compelled to bear a portion of the family expense even in those states which do not impose upon her a general obligation to sustain such charges. It is a general rule that the minor children have a right of demanding maintenance from the mother as well as from the father, though the former's liability is in most cases secondary to that of the latter.

There has been no such unanimity in granting the husband a right of demanding the necessary aliments from his wife. Most of the legislations, particularly in England and America, have rules for enforcing the husband's obligation to support the wife. The provisions may lead to the placing of the husband's property in the hands of trustees. They include criminal as well as civil penalties.[6] Many of the acts date back to the period in which the economic interests of the married woman were entirely in the control of the husband.

The English common law recognized no obligation on the part of the wife to support her husband out of her property. Such a provision would have been redundant under the old system. The husband was entitled to the substance of the wife's personal property and to the profits of her real estate. The law likewise secured him the privilege of controlling his wife's services and of collecting the proceeds

---

[5] France, C. C., 1448; Italy, C. C., 1423; Spain, C. C., 1434; La., C. C., 2434; Finland, Stat., Apl. 15, 1889, c. v, § 16; Basle, court determines the amount, Stat., Mch. 10, 1884, art. 41; Lucerne, restricted to income, Stat., Nov. 26, 1880, art. 22; *cf.* Prussia, A. L. R., ii. 1, § 262.

[6] It is possible in some states for a wealthy wife to obtain a divorce on the ground of lack of support.

arising from her labor. Aside from the substance of the wife's realty, the husband had absolute right to all of his wife's property. To-day, the husband is deprived of these extensive privileges, and is left with practically no legal rights of economic value as regards his wife or her property. His right to her services can no longer be enforced against her will.

Some of the Continental codes require the married woman to support her husband if his means are insufficient,[7] and similar provisions were incorporated in the English Married Women's Property Acts of 1870 and 1882.[8] The American states have been slow to accept this principle. Only a few legislations contain positive provisions making the wife liable for the support of her husband, and in all cases the husband's incapacity to support himself must be due to infirmity.[9] In a few cases the husband is given privileges in his wife's property in case she has abandoned him.[10]

Some evidence of a tendency to place the husband and wife upon a condition of equality with respect to obligations for support is to be found in the newer legislation regarding the effects of divorce. No part of the law regulating family relations in the United States is in such a chaotic state as that which provides for the judicial dissolution of the marriage and the effects of such dissolution. Statutory provisions in the respective states display a great lack of uniformity, and

---

[7] Germany, B. G., § 1360; Saxony, B. G., § 1637; Italy, C. C., 132; Spain, C. C., 143, 144; *cf.* Prussia, A. L. R., ii. 1, §262. In some of the states there is a general provision requiring married parties to render mutual assistance; France, C. C., 219; Prussia, A. L. R. ii. 1, § 174; Leuthold, *R. R.*, p. 59.

[8] Act, 33 & 34 Vict., c. 93, § 13; Act, 45 & 46 Vict., c. 75, § 20.

[9] Cal., C. C., 176; Idaho, R. S. 1887, § 2507; Mont., C. C., 1895, § 246; Nev., G. S., 1885, § 522.

[10] Iowa, Code, 1897, §§ 2220, 3158; Oklah., R. S., 1893, § 2975; Penn., Dig., 1883, p. 1348, §§ 51–55; Utah, R. S., 1898, § 1220.

in many cases are illogical and inequitable in character. This condition is due not only to the great extension of the grounds for divorce, but also to changes which have been effected in the matrimonial property relations.

Under the old system, alimony existed for the wife, generally without regard to the question of her innocence or guilt. Moreover, if the husband was the guilty party, he was required to restore the wife's property at once, while the wife retained her dower in his lands. If the husband obtained the divorce, he retained all or a portion of the property of the wife, while the latter lost all her rights in her husband's property. In all cases the husband was liable for the support and maintenance of the common children.

With the development of the separate property of the wife these provisions assumed an inequitable character. An innocent husband might be compelled to pay alimony, including the expenses of defending the suit for divorce, to a guilty wife possessed of independent means, while, on the other hand, he had ceased to possess property of the wife which he might use to assist him in defraying the expenses of the maintenance of the children and of the common household.

The states have not adopted the same methods for ameliorating this condition. In some, statutory provisions have made the wife, equally with the husband, liable for the maintenance of the minor children,[11] while in others such liability of the wife will attach only where she has been ad-

[11] Conn., G. S., 1888, § 2812; Ind., An. St., 1894, § 1058; Ky., Stat., 1894, § 2123; Me., R. S., 1883, c. 59, § 17; Minn., G. S., 1894, §§ 4801–4803; Miss., An. Code, 1892, § 1565; Mo., R. S., 1899, § 2926; Mont., C. C., 1895, § 191; Neb., C. S., 1891, § 1432; N. J., Rev., 1877, p. 317, § 19; N. D., R. C., 1895, § 2759; Ohio, R. S., 1891, § 5701, as amended by Statute, May 19, 1894, Acts, p. 348; S. D., C. L., 1887, § 2582; Utah, R. S., 1898, § 1212; Va., Code, 1887, § 2263; W. Va., Code, 1891, c. 64, § 11; Hawaii, C. L., 1884, §§ 1328, 1329; cf. Ariz., R. S., 1887, § 2114.

judged the guilty party.[12]   A few statutes provide that the
separate estate of the wife shall be taken into consideration,
and that alimony may be refused if she has sufficient property for her needs.[13]

Quite a number of the states have accepted the principle
of equal rights for both parties.   There is a general provision that alimony may be granted to the innocent party, or
the court is authorized to make such disposition of the property of the parties as under the circumstances will be just
and equitable.[14]   This is the position of the European legislations.[15]

A tendency has appeared in the newer legislations to
limit the amount which either party may receive to an alimentary pension payable only so long as it may be needed.
This is generally coupled with a proviso that the guilty
party shall restore, while the innocent party shall retain, all
economic benefits gained as a result of the marriage.

---

[12] Kans., G. S., 1889, § 4756; Mass., P. S., 1882, c. 146, § 27; N. H., P. S.,
1891, c. 175, § 13; Oklah., R. S., 1893, § 4550; Oreg., An. St., 1887, § 501;
Wis., An. St., 1889, § 2365; cf. England, Act, 20 and 21 Vict., c. 85, § 45.

[13] Ala., Code, 1896, § 1495; Cal., C. C., 142; Geo., Code, 1895, § 2458; Idaho,
R. S., 1887, § 2477; Mont., C. C., 1895, § 195; Tenn., Code, 1884, § 3326.

[14] Iowa, Code, 1897, §§ 3177-3180; Mass., P. S., 1882, c. 146, § 15; Nev.,
G. S., 1585, § 494; N. C., Code, 1883, § 1290; Ohio, R. S., 1891, §§ 5690-5701,
as amended by Statute, Feb. 9, 1893, Acts, p. 30, and Statute May 19, 1894, Acts,
p. 348; Oreg., An. St., 1887, § 501; R. I., G. L., 1896, c. 195, § 8; Vt., Stat.,
1894, § 2694; Va., Code, 1887, § 2263; Wash., C. P., 1891, § 771; W. Va.,
Code, 1891, c. 64, § 11; England, Act, 20 and 21 Vict., c. 85, § 45; cf. Ariz.,
R. S., 1887, § 2114; Cal., C. C., 146; Idaho, R. S., 1887, § 2480; Ill., An. St.,
1885, c. 68, ¶ 5.

[15] Germany, B. G., §§ 1578-1585; Prussia, A. L. R., ii., 1, §§ 783 *seq.*, 809
seq.; Saxony, B. G., §§ 1750, 1751; Austria, B. G., § 117; France, C. C., 299-301;
Italy, C. C., 156; Spain, C. C., 73; Basle, Stat., Mch. 10, 1884, art. 23; Lucerne,
Stat., Nov. 26, 1880, art. 25; Zürich, P. R. G., § 629 *seq.;* Switz., *Vorentwurf,*
170-172.

§ 44. *Liability for Debts.*

Under the rules of the English common law, the husband was liable for his wife's ante-nuptial and post-nuptial obligations, including those arising from torts as well as those proceeding from contracts.[1] The married women's property acts have affected this liability and practically abrogated it. When the husband ceased to receive economic benefits from the wife as a necessary result of the marriage, one of the chief grounds justifying his responsibility for her obligations disappeared.

The husband's liability did not rest alone upon the fact that he received property from the wife. He was liable even if he received nothing, while, on the other hand, his liability ceased at her death even if he had received all of her property. At the same time, it is beyond question that the chief explanation of the husband's release from such liability is to be found in the fact that the law does not accord him any right to his wife's property.

Another influence has grown out of the change in the legal economic position of the married woman. To-day the wife possesses property which, even during coverture, is liable to execution for the payment of her debts.

Most of the legislations take the position that where separate property obtains, neither married party is responsible for the obligations of the other except where these have been contracted for necessaries for the support of the family,[2] or in the sphere of an express or implied agency. In order to protect the wife's ante-nuptial creditors, a proviso has been introduced in some statutes making the husband liable to the extent of any property he may have received from the wife.[3]

---

[1] For character and extent of this obligation, see Schouler, *H. & W.*, Part iv, Chaps. ii, iii.   [2] *Cf. ante,* § 43.

[3] England and Ireland, Act, 33 and 34 Vict., c. 93, § 12, had provided an abso-

Particular provisions exist in some legislations respecting the obligations arising from the post-nuptial torts of the wife. A few of the American states retain the husband's common law liability,[4] but the majority of the legislations do not recognize any resposibility on the part of the husband except where the act was done under his coercion or authorizaiion or where he would be jointly liable if the marriage did not exist.[5]

lute exemption. This was repealed by Act, 37 and 38 Vict., c. 50, which introduced above rule; as between husband and wife her separate property is primarily liable, 45 and 46 Vict., c. 75, §§ 13–15; Scotland, Act, 40 and 41 Vict., c. 29, § 4; Ky., Stat., 1894, §2130; Col., An. St., 1891, § 3014; Geo., Code, 1895, § 2473; Ind., An, St., 1894, § 6970; Mo., R. S., 1899, § 4341; N. Y., Laws, 1896, c. 272, § 24; W. Va., Code, c. 66, § 11, as enacted by Acts, 1893, c. iii.

[4] Geo., Code, 1895, § 3817; N. M., C. L., § 1503; N. C., Code, 1883, § 1833; Wy., R. S., 1887, § 1565; *cf.* Del., R. C., 1893, c. 76, p. 600.

[5] Ala., Code, 1896, § 2525; Conn., G. S., 1888, § 984; Ill., An. St., 1885, c. 68, ¶ 4; Ind., An. St., 1894, §§ 6965, 6966; Iowa, Code, 1897, §§ 3151, 3156; Ky., Stat., 1894, § 2120; Me., R. S., 1884, c. 61, § 4; Md., Laws, 1898, c. 457, § 5; Mich., An. St., 1882, § 7714; Minn., Laws, 1897, c. 10; Mont., C. C., 1895, §§ 218, 226, 254; N, Y., Laws, 1896, c. 273, § 27; N. D., R. C., 1895, § 2770; Ohio, R. S., 1891, § 3115; Oklah., R. S. 1893, § 2972; Oreg., An. St., 1887, § 2996; R. I., G. L., 1896, c. 194, § 14; S. D., C. L., 1887, §2594; Utah, R. S., 1898, § 1204; Vt., Stat., 1894, §2648; Wash., G. S., 1891, § 1413; Wis., An. St., 1889, § 2969; Hawaii, Laws, 1888, c. xi, § 7; England, Act, 45 and 46, Vict., c. 75, §§ 1, 14, 24.

PART III.

SUCCESSION OF MARRIED PARTIES.

§ 45. *General Relation to Matrimonial Property Rights.*

Any general comparison of matrimonial property systems will be incomplete without a consideration of the mutual rights of inheritance of married parties. The converse is equally true. An examination of the provisions governing the succession of married parties reveals the greatest divergence among the various legislations, and it would be impossible to explain the differences without reference to the property relations of the parties during the marriage.

The history of the law of succession of married parties in a particular legislation often illustrates this close relationship. Thus, in the early Roman law, the wife has the same right of succession as the children. In legal terms this is explained by the fact that she is one of the agnatic family, one of the *sui heredes*. Its moral basis, however, reveals itself in the fact that the husband, in the marriage with *manus*, receives all that the wife possesses or acquires in the same way as he obtains the acquisitions of his children, hence she is of right entitled to the same share in his succession as is accorded to a child.

The rule of succession was confined in its application to the civil law marriage with *manus*. The woman who did not come under the marital power was not recognized as a wife (*mater familias*) in the strict sense of the civil law, and she could not claim the civil law rights which a wife possessed in the succession of her deceased husband. She did not become a member of his agnatic family.

The prætorian law, which introduced important modifications in the civil law of succession, did not accord any extensive privilege to the wife. The prætor brought about a development from the succession based upon agnatic or family organization to that resting upon cognate or blood relationship. The surviving married party, in so far as he did not possess a civil law right of succession, was postponed to all relatives of a degree capable of succeeding.

The explanation of this seeming harshness, in a legal system that was distinguished by its equitable character, is to be found in the fact that the relations of the husband and wife had, in general, come under the dotal system. The wife's property did not pass, as a result of the marriage, into the ownership of the husband. The *dos* and the *donatio propter nuptias* generally furnished the wife adequate provision for the contingency of the husband's prior death. Moreover, under the prætorian system, she had a right of succession to the property of her father and cognatic relatives. The later imperial legislation made provision for a widow in indigent circumstances. She was granted a fourth part of the estate of her husband, but if the decedent left three or more children she was restricted to a child's share. If the children were common to both parties the share was held in usufruct. This interest was not subject to the testamentary disposition of the husband.[1]

Teutonic law did not accord the wife a right of inheritance in the proper sense of the term.[2] But, as a result of the marriage, she acquired certain economic interests from her

---

[1] Sohm, *Inst.*, § 111.

[2] Heusler, *Inst.*, vol. ii, p. 421, *seq.*

husband or rights in his property which were in the nature of provisions for the future dissolution of the marriage.[3] In addition, where community of goods obtained, the widow received her share of the joint property or retained her rights in the community which was continued with the children (*fortgesetzte Gütergemeinschaft*). Where the marital administration and usufruct was the rule, the dotal property was returned to the widow as nearly as possible in the same condition as it existed at the time the husband received the same.

The English common law rules, while influenced by peculiar conditions, illustrate the same general principle. The wife is given no right of inheritance or claim to a distributive share in the estate of her deceased husband. But her dower right in the lands of her husband becomes consummate upon his death and she regains possession of her individual real property.

Modern systems of inheritance rest upon the principle of blood relationship. In all legislations, however, this general principle is modified by the recognition of an interest, great or small, of the surviving married party. This was the position which the Roman law was beginning to take at the time its development was checked. Modern legislations, in effect, recognize that the marriage establishes a bond between the parties similar to the ties of kinship. If the matrimonial property system contains adequate provision for the future of the survivor, the law of succession may disregard or but slightly emphasize such connection. On the other hand, if death immediately dissolves the matrimonial property relationships and leaves the survivor in the same economic position, so far as concerns the decedent, as at the beginning of the marriage, the law of inheritance will generally grant the former an interest in the latter's succession.

[3] *Widerlage, Witthum, Morgengabe. Cf.* Heusler, *Inst.*, vol. ii, pp. 370–376.

The modern legislation has also tended to place the married parties on a condition of equality in this matter. Provision is made for the surviving married party, and distinctions which were made according as the survivor was the husband or the wife, are gradually being eliminated. This interest may be a simple right of intestate succession, or it may be a legal portion which is not subject to testamentary disposition. The latter, moreover, may include only that which is necessary for subsistence, or it may extend to a distinct share in the succession of the decedent.

§ 46. *Intestate Succession.*

The French Civil Code was for a long period taken as the model by most of the states which recognized a community of property as the statutory system. This code originally postponed the surviving married party to all relatives of a degree capable of succeeding and to illegitimate children.[1] The theory was that the share of the survivor in the common property would constitute a sufficient provision, and he was not even accorded an alimentary pension.[2] The freedom of contract, however, permitted the severe restriction of the principle of community as well as the establishment of an entirely different system. Thus, it was possible that the survivor who possessed no individual property would find himself in reduced and even necessitous circumstances in case the decedent died intestate or failed to make proper provision in his will.

In France, as early as 1872,[3] an act was proposed which had for its object the extension of the successoral rights of

[1] C. C., 767; relatives up to the twelfth degree are capable of succession, *ibid.*, 755.

[2] *Cf., post*, § 48.

[3] Viollet, *Précis*, p. 698, note 3.

the surviving married party.[4] Nearly twenty years elapsed before the legislative sanction was finally obtained in a statute of March 9, 1891.[5] The French legislature was influenced by the fact that other states whose legislations were based upon the Code Napoléon, had modified its provisions in the interests of the surviving spouse. The most recent instance of such legislation is the Belgian statute of November 20, 1896, which modifies Article 767 of the Civil Code in accordance with the same general principles that influenced the French act of 1891.[6]

As a rule, the interest of the survivor in the intestate succession of the deceased spouse is limited to a right of usufruct for life where issue or heir exists. If there are no heirs capable of succeeding, the surviving married party takes all in full ownership. The amount of the property covered by the usufruct will be affected by the number and degree of the existing heirs.[7] The states in which the

[4] Earlier statutes had granted the widow certain successoral rights in particular kinds of property: Right to dispose of artistic and literary products of decedent, Stat., Apl. 8, 1854, *Bull. des lois*, xi. sér., vol. 3, p. 869; Stat., July 14, 1866, art, 1, *Bull. des lois*, xi. sér., vol. 28, p. 61; widows of pensioned officials are in certain cases entitled to a continuation of a certain proportion of the pension, Stat., June 9, 1853, arts. 13, 14, *Bull des lois*, xi. sér., vol. 1, p. 989; Stat., Apl. 11, 1831, art. 19, *Bull des lois*, ix. sér., vol. 2, p. 166; Stat., Apl. 18, 1831, art. 19, *Bull des lois*, ix. sér., vol. 2, p. 239.

[5] *An. fran.*, vol. 11, p. 147 *seq.*; *cf. An. étran.*, vol. 4, p. 497, note 1.

[6] *An. étran.*, vol. 26, p. 498 *seq.*

[7] France, 1/4, if issue exists, but not to exceed child's part if issue is of previous marriage; 1/2, if no issue exists (C. C., 767 as amended by Stat., Mch. 9, 1891, art. 1, *An. fran.*, vol. 11, p. 147); Belgium, share of legitimate child if issue exists, but not to exceed 1/4 if issue is of previous marriage; 1/2, if no issue, but ascendants or brother or sister or their descendants; all, if only other collaterals exist (Stat., Nov. 20, 1896, § 1, *An. étran.*, vol. 26, p. 498); Spain, legal portion of each child if issue exists; 1/3, if no issue, but ascendants; 1/2, in other cases (C. C., 834-837, 952); Geneva, 1/2, if legitimate issue exists; 1/4 in ownership, if no legitimate issue; 1/2 in ownership, if no descendants, father or mother or their descendants (C. C., 767 as amended by Stat., Sept. 5, 1874, *An. étran.*, vol. 4, p.

system of dowry is the statutory regime, have adopted similar provisions for intestate succession.[8]

The provisions, at least so far as concerns community systems, where issue exists, are extensions of matrimonial property law rather than proper hereditary shares.[9] The survivor is given, in addition to his share in the common property, a usufruct for life over a certain part of the shares falling to the issue of the marriage.[10] Upon the death of the survivor, the descendants recover the usufruct of the property of which they have previously possessed only the title.

The states recognizing marital administration and usufruct as the statutory system do not follow this principle. In this system, the death of either party brings about an immediate dissolution of the matrimonial property relations, and the survivor does not retain any privileges in the property of the decedent. The law of succession, accordingly, supplements the matrimonial property law. The survivor is generally accorded an hereditary share in ownership even

499); Basle City, survivor postponed to relatives of fifth degree, but he has during minority of children the usufruct of their shares in the succession (Stat., Mch. 10, 1884, art. 48); La., common issue's heritable share of common property; intestate's share of community if no issue or ascendants exist (C. C., 915–917). The other American states that have introduced community of property provide a substantial right of intestate succession for the survivor (see below, note 19).

[8] Austria, usufruct of child's share not to exceed ¼; ¼ in ownership, if no issue exists (B. G., §§ 757–759); Italy, usufruct of child's share, the survivor being counted in the number of children; ⅓ in ownership, if no legitimate issue, but natural children, ascendants, brother or sister or their descendants exist; if natural children and ascendants come together, the share is limited to ¼; ⅔ in ownership, if none of foregoing, but relatives up to sixth degree exist (C. C., 753–755).

[9] *Cf.* community continued between survivor and common children, *ante*, § 23, (e).

[10] In European legislation, the surviving husband has a right of usufruct over the shares of minor children, and where, as in the German code, parental instead of paternal authority is established, the widow possesses such right. *Cf. Motive,* vol. 5, p. 368.

where issue exists, though the extent of such share is generally affected by the number and degree of the existing relatives of the decedent.[11]

The legislations which recognize separate property as the statutory system likewise accord a right of succession to the survivor of the marriage. In Russia, this is fixed at one-fourth of the movable and one-seventh of the immovable property of the decedent, and obtains without regard to the existence of issue of the marriage.[12]

In England and the United States, the determination of the hereditary rights of the surviving married party has been complicated by many conditions. The development of the new matrimonial property systems has not been perfected. Institutions that are the products of the earlier customs have, in many cases, been carried over, without modification, into the new system. Moreover, the distinction between the succession to real and personal property, which was empha-

---

[11] Germany, $\frac{1}{4}$, if descendants; $\frac{1}{2}$, if no descendants, but parents, or their descendants, or grandparents; all, in other cases (B. G., § 1931; *cf.* § 1932); Prussia, child's part not to exceed $\frac{1}{4}$; $\frac{1}{3}$, if no descendants, but brother or sister or their children; $\frac{1}{2}$, if none of foregoing, but other relatives up to sixth degree; all, in other cases (A. L. R., ii, 1, §§ 621–627; *cf.* §§ 628–630); Saxony, $\frac{1}{4}$, if descendants; $\frac{2}{3}$, if no descendants, but adopted or natural children; $\frac{1}{2}$, if none of foregoing, but brother or sister or their descendants, parents or grandparents; all, in other cases (B. G., §§ 2049–2053); Lucerne, $\frac{1}{4}$, in usufruct, if descendants; $\frac{1}{4}$, in ownership, if only heirs of second class; $\frac{1}{3}$, in ownership, if none of foregoing; $\frac{1}{2}$, in ownership, if there are no heirs capable of succession (Lardy, *Législations Suisses*, p. 145); Zürich, $\frac{1}{8}$ in ownership or $\frac{1}{2}$ in usufruct, if descendants; $\frac{1}{4}$, in ownership or all, in usufruct, if only parents or their descendants; $\frac{1}{2}$, in ownership and other $\frac{1}{2}$, in usufruct, if only grandparents or their descendants; $\frac{3}{4}$, in ownership and other $\frac{1}{4}$ in usufruct, if only greatgrandparents or their descendants; all, in ownership, if no relatives capable of succession (P. R. G., §§ 901, 905; *cf.* § 900); Glaris, if survivor elects to turn all of his individual property into the succession of the intestate, he will receive a child's share, and if no children, $\frac{1}{2}$ of such succession. Otherwise, he receives no share in the succession (L. B. ii, arts. 303, 304).

[12] Leuthold, *R. R.*, p. 79; Lehr, *Droit Russe*, p. 424.

sized under the influence of feudal ideas, has been continued to a large extent in the modern rules governing the succession of the surviving married party. Finally, the distinction between the successoral rights of husband and wife is retained to a greater degree than in other countries, though the tendency to eliminate the same is quite apparent.

At common law the widow had no hereditary or distributive share in the real or personal estate of her deceased husband. On the other hand, the husband was entitled to all of his deceased wife's personal property, subject to the payment of debts. The widow had her dower right and the husband, if the necessary condition had been fulfilled, was entitled to his tenancy by the curtesy.[13]

The law affecting personal property was modified by an act of the seventeenth century, which gave the widow a share in the intestate's personal estate of one-third, if the decedent left children, and otherwise of one-half.[14] This was a general statute of distributions, but was not intended to apply to the estates of married women.[15] No further change in the rules of succession of married parties has been made in England, except that a statute, enacted in 1890, gives the widow all of the personal estate up to the value of £500 and her distributive share in the residue when the husband dies intestate, without issue.[16] Aside from the restricted interests of dower and curtesy,[17] neither party has any hereditary right to the real estate of the other, and the

[13] *Ante*, § 25.

[14] Act, 22 and 23, Car. II, c. 10, §§ v, and vi, enacted only for seven years, but re-enacted for similar period by 30 Car. II, Stat., 1, c. 6, and made permanent by 1 Jac. II, c. 17, cl. 17, § 5.

[15] To remove any doubt on this score, a section was incorporated in the "Statute of Frauds" (29 Car. II, c. 3, § xxv), declaring that the husband should enjoy the same rights as before the passing of the statute of distributions.

[16] Act, 53 and 54 Vict., c. 29.

[17] *Ante*, § 40.

same will escheat to the State in the absence of heirs and of testamentary disposition.[18]

At first glance, the laws of succession in the United States present a bewildering mass of divergent rules. Aside from the western states and territories that have followed the Code of California, it is difficult to find two legislations that agree in their provisions respecting the succession of married parties. Upon closer examination, however, certain tendencies appear that give promise of greater unity and uniformity.

There is substantial unanimity in according the survivor an interest in the succession of the predeceased intestate married party. This may be a share in the estate as a whole, or it may be restricted to the real or to the personal estate of the decedent. The most significant feature, from the standpoint of matrimonial property relations, is the tendency to place the husband and wife on an equality so far as respects the share of either in the intestate succession of the other.

More than three-fifths of the legislations have established such substantial equality, the interest in general being defined as one existing for the benefit of the surviving married party.[19] While the right to such share arises without

[18] The same appears to be true of one-half of the husband's personalty, where relatives entitled to a distributive share do not exist.

[19] Dower and courtesy are sometimes recognized, in addition to the intestate share, see *ante*, § 40. Arizona, if issue, ⅓, but only for life in lands; if no issue, but father or mother, all of personal estate and ½ of real estate in fee; if no issue or parent, all (R. S., 1887, § 1460).

California, if issue, child's share, not to be less than ⅓; if no issue, but parent, brother or sister, ½; if none of foregoing, all (C. C., § 1386).

Colorado, if issue, ½; if no issue, all (An. St., 1891, § 1524).

Connecticut, if issue, ½; if no issue, all up to $2,000 and ½ of residue (G. S., 1888, § 623, as amended by Laws, 1895, c. 217).

Florida, if issue, child's share; if no issue, all (R. S., 1892, §§ 1820, 1833).

Georgia, if issue, child's share, but widow's share not to be less than $1/5$; if no issue, all (Code, 1895, §§ 3354, 3355).

regard to the issue of children from the marriage, the amount of the interest increases in proportion to the non-

Idaho, same as California (R. S., 1887, § 5705).

Illinois, if issue, ⅓ of personal estate; if no issue, but kindred, ½ of real estate and all of personal estate; if no kindred, entire estate (An. St., 1885, c. 39, ¶ 1).

Indiana, if issue, ⅓, but wife entitled to claim child's share; if no issue, but parent, ¾, and if estate does not exceed $1,000, all; if no issue or parent, all (An. St,, 1894, §§ 2640–2644, 2650, 2651).

Iowa, if issue, ⅓; if no issue, but parents or their heirs, ½; if none of foregoing, all (Code, 1897, §§ 3362, 3366, 3376, 3377, 3382).

Kansas, same as Colorado (G. S., 1889, §§ 2599, 2611, 2619, 2622).

Maine, if issue, dower in real estate and ⅓ of personal estate; if no issue, but kindred, dower increased to ½ if estate is solvent and same share is taken in personal estate; if no kindred, entire estate in ownership (R. S., 1883, c. 75, §§ 1, 9, c. 103, § 14).

Michigan, if issue, dower and curtesy (*cf. ante,* § 40, note 16) in real estate and child's share, not to be less than ⅓ in personal estate; if no issue, but parent, brother or sister or their descendants, ½ of real estate in fee and all of personal estate up to $1,000 and ½ of residue; if none of foregoing entire estate (An. St., 1882, § 5772 as amended by Pub. Acts, 1889, no. 168, p. 193, § 5847).

Minnesota, if issue. ⅓; if no issue, all (G. S., 1894, §§ 4471, 4477).

Mississippi, same as Florida (An. Code, 1892, § 1545).

Missouri, if issue, dower and curtesy in real estate and, for widow, child's share in personal estate; if no issue, but parent, brother or sister of their descendants, ½ of entire estate in ownership; if none of foregoing, all (R. S., 1899, §§ 2908, 2937–2939.)

Montana, same as California (C. C., 1895, § 1852).

Nebraska, if issue, child's share not less than ⅓; if no issue, but kindred, ½; if no kindred, all (C. S., 1891, §§ 1124, 1235).

Nevada, if issue, child's share not less than ⅓; if no issue, all (Laws, 1897, c. 106, § 259).

New Hampshire, if issue, ⅓, but if issue of wife is by former marriage, surviving husband takes only a life estate in ⅓, unless he is entitled to curtesy; if no issue, ½ (P. S., 1891, c. 195, §§ 10–13).

New Mexico, if issue, ¼; if no issue, all (C. L., 1897, §§ 2031, 2033).

North Dakota, same as California, except that if no issue, but parent, brother, or sister, survivor takes all up to $5,000 and ½ of residue (R. C., 1895, § 3742).

Ohio, if issue, dower in real estate and all of personal estate up to $400 and ⅓ of residue; if no issue, entire estate, but limited to a life interest in ancestral real property if intestate leaves kindred of blood of ancestor from whom such property was derived (R. S., 1891, §§ 4158, 4160, 4176).

existence of descendants or of near relatives of the decedent.

Oklahoma, same as California (R. S., 1893, § 6261).

Oregon, if issue, dower and curtesy in real estate and ⅓ of personal estate; if
no issue, entire estate in ownership (An. St., 1887, § 3098, as amended by Stat.,
Feb. 25, 1889, Acts, p. 72, § 3099, as amended by Stat., Feb. 22, 1893, Acts, p.
195).

South Carolina, if issue, ⅓; if no issue, but lineal ancestor, brother or sister,½;
if none of the foregoing, but kindred, ⅔; if no kindred, all (C. S. L., 1893,
§§ 1980, 2166).

South Dakota, same as California (G. L., 1887, § 3401).

Texas, same as Arizona, except that issue of parent will limit right of survivor
in same degree as parent (R. S., 1895, art. 1689).

Utah, same as North Dakota (R. S., 1898, § 2828).

Vermont, if issue, ⅓ of real estate in fee, but husband's right is limited to lands
of which both parties are seized in right of the wife, and surviving wife takes in addition ⅓ of personal estate as part of widow's allowance; if no issue, but kindred,
entire estate up to $2,000 and ½ of residue; if no kindred, all (Pub. Acts, 1896,
no. 44, §§ 1, 2, 15, Stat., 1894, §§ 2418, 2419, 2546 and 2544, as amended by Pub.
Acts, 1886, no. 45, § 1.

Washington, if issue, child's share in real estate, not less than ⅓, and ½ of
personal estate; if no issue, but parent, brother or sister, ½ of real estate and all
personal estate; if none of the foregoing, entire estate (G. S., 1881, §§ 1480,
1495).

Wisconsin, if issue, dower and curtesy (*cf. ante*, § 40, note 12), in real estate,
and for widow child's part in personal estate; if no issue, entire estate in ownership (An. St., 1889, §§ 2270, 3935).

Wyoming, if issue, dower; if no issue, ¾, but if estate does not exceed $10,000
in value, all (R. S., 1887, § 2221).

Hawaii, if issue, dower; if no issue, but parents or their descendants, ½ in
ownership; if none of foregoing, all (C. L., 1884, § 1448, as amended by Laws,
1896, no. 47).

Massachusetts may be placed in this class, as the tendency towards equalization is evident. Surviving husband takes: if issue, curtesy and ½ of personal
estate; if no issue, all of real estate up to value of $5,000 in fee and life interest
in residue, and entire personal estate; if no kindred, entire estate in ownership.
Widow takes: if issue, dower and ⅓ of personal estate; if no issue, but kindred,
all of real estate up to value of $5,000 in fee and life interest in residue of which
husband died seized, or the same amount and dower in other lands, and all of
the personal estate up to value of $5,000 and ½ of residue above value of $10,000;
if no kindred, entire estate in ownership (P. S., 1882, c. 124, §§ 1, 2, c. 135, § 3
as amended by Acts, 1882, c. 141, and Acts, 1885, c. 276).

It is a curious fact that while the common law rule of curtesy favors the propagation of issue, some of the modern rules of succession may produce contrary effects, as where the survivor is given a child's share. A tendency has appeared to accord the survivor a definite share or, where he is given a child's share, to place a minimum upon the same.[20] It may be noted that in the great majority of those legislations that recognize equal rights of succession for the husband and wife, the distinction between the share in the real and in the personal estate has been abolished.

Most of the remaining states retain the common law rules respecting the succession to real property. The survivor is generally postponed to all heirs or kindred, and in some cases excluded entirely, the property escheating to the state.[21] It must be kept in mind, however, that in these

[20] *Cf.* preceding note and rules in German, Saxon and Russian codes, *ante*, notes 11, 12.

[21] Alabama, Code, 1896, § 1453, but husband has life interest in real estate of intestate wife (*ibid.*, § 2534).

Arkansas, Dig. Stat., 1894, § 2476, but if no issue, widow may take, as against collaterals, ½, and, as against creditors, ⅓ in fee of non-ancestral real property, of which husband died seized and a life interest in proportionate amounts of the ancestral real property (*ibid.*, § 2542).

Delaware, if no issue, husband takes ½ of real estate, subject to debts, while widow takes a life interest in same amount, and if there are no heirs or kindred she takes such interest in the entire real estate (Laws, vol. 14, c. 550, § 5 in R. C., 1893, c. 76).

Kentucky, Stat., 1894, § 1393, ¶ 9.

Maryland, P. G. L., 1888, art. 46, § 23.

New Jersey, Rev., 1877, p. 297, § 6.

New York, a statute of Mch. 28, 1895 (Acts, c. 171), provided that the surviving wife should inherit the same share of an intestate's real estate as the nearest lineal descendant, and that if no issue existed she should inherit all of such estate. This Act was to go into effect on Jan. 1, 1896, but was repealed by a statute of June 14, 1895 (Acts, c. 1022), which re-established the former rules of inheritance.

North Carolina, Code, 1883, § 1281.

Pennsylvania, if no issue but kindred, widow takes ½ for life (Dig., 1883, pp. 929, 932, §§ 1–3, 6, 28).

legislations the matrimonial property rights of dower and curtesy have generally been retained, and in some cases the husband's interest has been made the same as that of the wife. All of these states, following the English statute of distribution, grant the wife a share in the personal estate of the intestate husband. This interest is usually the one-third or one-half of the English statute, but some of the legislations have departed from the general rule by making the share of the surviving husband the same as that which is accorded the widow.[22]

Rhode Island, G. L., 1896, c. 216, § 4.
Tennessee, Code, 1884, § 3272.
Virginia, Code, 1887, § 2548.
West Virginia, Code, 1891, c. 78, § 1.
District of Columbia, Acts of Maryland, 1786, c. 45, § 2.

[22] Alabama, husband, ½; wife, child's part, not less than $1/_5$, and if no children, all (Code, 1896, §§ 2534, 1462).

Arkansas, if issue, wife takes ⅓ absolutely; if no issue, she takes ½ as against collaterals, and ⅓ as against creditors; if no kindred, survivor takes all (Dig. Stat., 1894, §§ 2541, 2542, 2476).

Delaware, husband takes child's share, and if no issue, all; wife takes ⅓, if issue, ½, if no issue but kindred, and all, if no kindred (Laws, 1895, c. 207, § 1, R. C., 1893, c. 89, § 32).

Kentucky, husband takes all; wife takes ⅓, if issue, ½, if no issue, but kindred and all, if no kindred (Stat., 1894, § 1403); § 2132 of the Statutes, which applies to testate as well as intestate succession, conflicts with foregoing section. It gives surviving married party ½ of personal estate of testator or intestate.

Maryland, survivor takes ⅓, if issue; ½, if no issue, but parent, brother, sister, nephew or niece; otherwise, all (P. G. L., 1888, arts. 120–122, as amended by Laws, 1898, c. 331, § 2).

New Jersey, husband takes all; wife takes ⅓, if issue; ½, if no issue (Rev., 1877, pp. 784, 785, §§ 147, 148).

New York, survivor takes: ⅓, if issue; ½, if no issue, but parent; if no issue or parent, but brother, sister, nephew or niece, all, if it does not exceed $2,000, and if value is greater, ½ plus $2,000; in other cases, all (R. S., 1889, part ii, c. ii, §§ 75, 79.

North Carolina, husband takes all; wife takes: child's part not less than ⅓; if no issue, ½; if no kindred, all (Code, 1883, §§ 1479, 1478 as amended by Laws, 1893, c. 82, § 1).

Pennsylvania, husband takes child's share, and if no issue, all; wife takes: if

§ 47. *Legal Portion.*

The fundamental idea at the basis of intestate, as well as of testamentary succession, is that of effectuating the intention of the decedent. The legislative body creates an order of succession which it is presumed would have been established by the deceased had he left a legal testament. In general, therefore, the rules of succession established by the legislature apply only in the absence of testament. But there are other rules that override the will of the deceased. While the individual is accorded the right of disposing of his property by testament, he will not be permitted to do so to the injury of those whose relation to him is such as to justify them in expecting a portion in the succession. The law generally provides that a certain proportion of the share which such person would have in the intestate succession shall be a legal portion, and shall not be subject to testamentary disposition. If the decedent leaves a will and fails to make proper provision for the parties entitled thereto, the latter will be able to claim their legal portion in the succession.[1] The legislature gives legal expression to the moral

issue, ⅓; if no issue, but kindred, ½; if no kindred, all (Dig., 1883, pp. 929–932, §§ 1–5, 28).

Rhode Island, husband takes all; wife, same as in Pennsylvania (G. L., 1896, c. 219, § 9, c. 194, § 9, c. 216, §§ 4, 9).

Tennessee, husband takes all at common law; wife takes child's share, and if no issue, all (Code, 1884, § 3278).

Virginia, same as in Rhode Island (Code, 1887, § 2557).

West Virginia, survivor takes ⅓, if issue, and all, if no issue (Code, 1891, c. 78, § 9).

District of Columbia, husband takes all at common law; wife takes, if issue, ⅓, if no issue, but parent, brother or sister or their descendants, ½; in other cases, all (Maryland, Acts, 1798, c. 101, part 11).

[1] This is not an absolute right, but is capable of being defeated when the conduct of the party entitled has been such as to justify his disinheritance. The statutes generally provide under what conditions one may be deprived of his legal portion.

right which certain heirs have to a share in the estate of the decedent.

The legal portion (*Pflichttheil ; portion légitime*) obtains very generally in the European continental countries, but has not received any extensive recognition in England or the United States aside from the succession of married parties. It may be noted, however, that so far as concerns the United States, at least, the numerous, and, in some instances, disgraceful cases of judicial breaking of wills on the ground of insanity, testify to the operation of the same principle. The courts, in effect, declare that no sane person can be presumed to have intended to disinherit those standing in close relationship to him. The fiction of insanity was at the basis of the Roman rule governing the claim to a legal portion as against the testamentary dispositions of the decedent.[2] It may be anticipated that the English law, following the example of other legislations, will ultimately give a rational definition of the legal portion of descendants, *etc.*

While the principle of the legal portion has received general acceptance in continental legislations, its application, in many instances, has been limited to those standing in blood relationship. The Roman law, in the time of Justinian, was just beginning to recognize the successoral rights of married parties. The principle of the legal portion was not extended to them though the provision for the poor widow was of this nature.[3]

The states recognizing a community form of matrimonial property relations have been slow to recognize a right of the surviving married party to a legal portion even when, in default of all other heirs, such survivor would be called to the intestate succession. When these legislations accorded the

---

[2] Sohm, *Inst.*, § 113.

[3] *Cf. ante*, § 45, *post*, § 48.

survivor an intestate right of succession as against all heirs,[4] they did not give it the character of a legal portion.[5]   It was not the object of the legislator to provide a share for the survivor, but to carry out the intention of the decedent by creating an order of succession which it was presumed the intestate would have established had he not forgotten or neglected to make a will.   Thus, these statutes generally require the surviving spouse to count towards his intestate share everything that he has received by way of donation from the decedent, whether the same has come to him as a result of the contract of marriage or otherwise.   Where the decedent has clearly manifested his intention by a written testament, the necessity for the application of the statute ceases to exist.   The Spanish code furnishes an exception to this class of legislations in according the surviving spouse the same share in case of testate as of intestate succession.[6]

Of the legislations accepting the system of dowry, the Italian code makes the share of the survivor substantially the same as in Spain by providing a right of usufruct[7] as a legal portion, while the Austrian[8] follows the principle of the Roman law.

The codes recognizing marital administration and usufruct as the statutory system, accord the surviving married party a substantial legal portion.   In general, the amount is fixed

[4] *Cf. ante*, § 46.

[5] This is true of the American states which recognize community of property, though the liberal grants of rights in the homestead and allowance for support have created a substantial legal portion.   *Cf. post*, § 48.

[6] C. C., 834–837, but if no heirs exist, the legal portion will not be the entire estate, which is the share in case of intestacy, but only $\frac{1}{2}$ in usufruct.

[7] Of a child's share, the survivor being counted in the number of children; of $\frac{1}{4}$, if no issue, but ascendants; of $\frac{1}{3}$, if no issue or ascendants (C. C., 812–814); *cf.* La., C. C., 2382.

[8] B. G., § 796.

at a certain part of the share which the survivor would take in case of intestate succession.[9]

Among the separate property legislations, Russia provides a legal portion,[10] while in England the principle has not received statutory recognition.[11]

So far as regards the application of the principle of the legal portion to the succession of married parties, the American states have gone farther than most of the European legislations. The recognition of the legal portion in positive legislation is almost entirely confined to the husband and wife. This apparently curious fact finds its explanation in the close relation existing between matrimonial property relations and the law of inheritance. Dower and curtesy are forms of legal portion. When the principle of the legal portion commenced to develop in America, the interest of the wife was the chief consideration, as the husband's marital property rights gave him an adequate share. Since he has been deprived of this interest, the tendency has appeared to accord him a legal portion of the same general character as that which is possessed by the wife.

Two-fifths of the American legislations recognize a legal portion for the survivor and in most of these the share of the surviving husband is the same as that which is taken by a widow.[12] A tendency appears to make the legal portion

[9] Germany, ½, B. G., § 2303; Prussia, ½, A. L. R., ii, 1, § 631; Saxony, if issue, all; if no issue, but heirs of second or third order of succession, ⅔; in other cases, ½ (B. G., §§ 2565, 2578–2580); Lucerne, all of intestate share taken where issue exists (Lardy, *Législations Suisses*, p. 146); Zürich, ¾ (P. R. G., § 974).

[10] Intestate share in all except acquisitions, which are subject to testamentary disposition (Leuthold, *R. R.*, pp. 79, 80; Lehr, *Droit Russe*, pp. 424–426).

[11] Even the widow's dower has been deprived of this character. *Cf. ante*, § 40, Marriage settlements frequently make provision for the survivor.

[12] Colorado, ½ of estate (An. St., 1891, §§ 3010, 3011).
Connecticut, life interest in ⅓ of estate (G. S., 1888, § 623).
Illinois, if issue, dower and intestate share in personalty; if no issue, may elect

equal to the intestate share, with a general proviso that it
shall not exceed a certain proportion of the estate. The
share is generally large, in some cases extending to one-half
of the entire estate in succession. This represents an extreme position, which is apt to be modified in the interests
of children. Moreover, the principle of the legal portion
does not require that a married party shall be compelled
to confer such a large part of his property upon one whose
conduct may have been objectionable, or who possesses ade-

in lieu of above, ½ of entire estate after payment of debts (An. St., 1885, c. 41,
¶¶ 10, 12).

Indiana, ⅓ of estate (An. St., 1894, §§ 2640, 2642, 2648, 2649).

Iowa, ⅓ of estate (Code, 1897, §§ 3362, 3366, 3376).

Kansas, ½ of estate (G. S., 1889, § 7239).

Kentucky, dower and ½ of personal estate (Stat., 1894, § 2132),

Maine, 'dower (R. S., 1883, c. 103, §§ 10, 14).

Maryland, dower and ⅓ of personal estate (P. G. L., 1888, art. 93, §§ 292, 293,
Laws, 1898, c. 331, § 3).

Massachusetts, substantially intestate share in real estate; in personal estate,
husband entitled to ½ and wife takes intestate share, except that if it exceeds
$10,000 in value, she receives only that amount and the income during life of res-
idue (P. S., 1882, c. 127, § 18, c. 147, § 6, as amended by Acts, 1885, c. 225, § 1, and
Acts, 1887, c. 290, § 2).

Minnesota, intestate share in real estate (G. S., 1894, §§ 4471, 4472).

Mississippi, intestate share not to exceed ½ (An. Code, 1892, § 4496).

Missouri, substantially intestate share not to exceed that taken where kindred
exists (R. S., 1899, §§ 2937–2939, Act, Mch. 2, 1895, Laws, p. 169).

Montana, husband, ⅓ of estate; wife, dower and, if no issue, ½ of real estate
in fee (C. C., 1895, §§ 255, 236, 1703).

Nebraska, intestate share (G. S., 1891, §§ 1124, 1235).

New Hampshire, intestate share, or dower or curtesy and intestate share in personal estate (P. S., 1891, c. 195, §§ 10–13, c. 186, § 13).

Ohio, intestate share (R. S., 1891, § 5963).

Pennsylvania, dower and curtesy and intestate share in personal estate (Dig.,
1883, p. 632, §§ 3, 5, pp. 1153, 1154, §§ 2, 6, Laws, 1893, p. 345, § 5).

Vermont, substantially intestate share not to exceed that taken where kindred
exists (Stat., 1894, § 2544, as amended by Laws, 1896, no. 45, § 1).

West Virginia, intestate share not to exceed that taken where issue exists (Code,
1891, c. 78, § 11).

quate individual resources. A few of the American states
have confined the legal portion to the wife.[13]

The legislations which do not accord a legal portion in the
strict sense of the term, divide themselves into two classes.
The first class includes those which recognize a community
of acquisitions, where the survivor takes his share in the
common property and is sometimes given special privileges
in the portion of the common property which falls to the
decedent.[14]. In the other class, the matrimonial property
rights of dower, and, in most cases, curtesy, continue to be
recognized.[15] Moreover, the liberal provisions which very
generally obtain for the support of the widow or survivor,
have the character of a legal portion.

§ 48. *Provision for the Support of the Survivor.*

Under all systems of matrimonial property relations, except where perfect community of all property obtains, it is
possible that the death of one party may seriously affect the
position of the other. Where the household expenses have
been defrayed largely, if not entirely, out of the property of
the decedent, the survivor, in the absence of suitable provision, may be compelled materially to alter his mode of liv-

[13] Alabama, dower and intestate share in personalty (Code, 1896, § 4259).

Arkansas, same as Alabama (Dig. Stat., 1894, §§ 2541, 2542).

Florida, dower in real estate; of personalty, if issue, $\frac{1}{3}$; if no issue, $\frac{1}{2}$ absolutely (R. S., 1892, §§ 1830, 1831).

Michigan, dower, or intestate share up to $5,000, and $\frac{1}{2}$ of residue (An. St.,
1882, § 5824).

North Carolina, intestate share (Code, 1883, § 2109).

Tennessee, dower and child's share, not to exceed $\frac{1}{3}$ of personalty (Code,
1884, §§ 3251, 3252).

Utah, $\frac{1}{3}$ of real estate, or intestate share in entire estate (R. S., 1898, §§ 2731,
2827).

Virginia, intestate share of personal estate (Code, 1887, § 2559).

[14] *Cf. ante,* § 24, notes 13–17.

[15] *Cf.* references, *ante,* § 40.

ing, and may even be unable to secure the necessary subsistence. Such deplorable spectacles are opposed to the
moral idea of marriage, and have led to the establishment of
the legal portion for married parties. The principle applies with added force to survivors who are in indigent circumstances. At the least, they should be entitled to the
necessary alimentary support, under the same circumstances
as they could have claimed it during the marriage.

This principle has come to be generally accepted in those
legislations which do not accord a legal portion to the surviving married party. The Code Napoléon did not recognize this right for the survivor.[1] The movement to incor-
porate this principle in the French Code was carried on for
many years in connection with the attempt to accord the
survivor a share in the succession of an intestate married
party. Both principles were finally accepted in the statute
of March 9, 1891.[2] The recent Belgian statute, which introduced the intestate share of a surviving married party, has
likewise followed the French statute in establishing the claim
of such survivor to alimentary support.[3]

The succession of the deceased married party owes maintenance to the survivor, provided the latter is in want
thereof.[4] If the survivor has sufficient individual means, he
can not claim such alimentary provision, nor can he do so if
his intestate share in the succession is sufficient for his needs.

Where the system of dowry obtains, the widow is entitled

[1] The claim which the Roman law gave to the poor widow, had obtained in the
pays d'écrit, but it was not admitted into the code. The Louisiana Civil Code
retains the Roman rule, but extends it so as to apply to the survivor who is in
need (C. C., 2382).

[2] *Cf. ante*, § 46.   [3] *Ibid.*

[4] France, C. C., 205, as amended by Stat., Mch. 9, 1891, art. 2, *An. fran.*, vol.
II, pp. 153, 154; Belgium, C. C., 205, as amended by Stat., Nov. 20, 1896, art.
2, *An. étran.*, vol. 26, pp. 502, 503; Austria, B. G., § 796.

to lodging for one year, and mourning vestments at the expense of the husband's succession.[5]

It is in the American states that the provision for the survivor has received the greatest acceptance and development. The general provision is that if the estate is insolvent, the personal property, exempt from execution, shall be set aside for the benefit of the widow or survivor. Similar provisions entitle such party to claim the absolute property of the homestead or its use for life or during widowhood.[6]

· These measures are natural corollaries to the exemption laws, and must be justified by similar considerations. This condition does not exist where the widow or survivor possesses separate property, or where the estate of the decedent is solvent, and the legal portion or intestate share of the survivor is sufficient for suitable support. Notwithstanding these facts, many of the states grant the allowance in addition to the legal portion or intestate share, and do not take into consideration the necessities of the person to whom the same is accorded. In some cases the amount exempted is quite large, and the interests of heirs and creditors are sacrificed without justification. Some of the statutes, however, expressly enact that the provision shall be deducted from the distributive share or legal portion, while others make it dependent upon the necessities of the party entitled. It may be anticipated that future revisions will tend to restrict the provision to that which is essential for alimentary support.

The original purpose of the legislation was to ensure provision for the widow. Thus, many of the statutes restrict

[5] France, C. C., 1570; Italy, C. C., 1415; La., C. C., 2374; *cf.* Spain, C. C., 1379; Austria, B. G., § 796.

[6] Minor children are usually granted an interest in such exempted property.

the allowance[7] and the use or ownership of the homestead[8] to the widow and, in some cases, the minor children. The tendency towards equalization of the parties, which has followed the establishment of separate property, is also manifested in this connection. It is aimed to accord the surviving husband the same rights in his deceased wife's property as the widow possesses in the estate of her deceased husband. Accordingly, in a large number of legislations the provisions respecting an allowance[9] and the disposition of the

[7] Ala., Code, 1896, §§ 2072, 2073; Ark., Dig. Stat., 1894, §§ 3, 73; Col., An. St., 1891, §§ 1534, 1536; Conn., G. S., 1888, §§ 574, 605; Del., R. C., 1893, c. 111, Laws, vol. 15, c. 479; Fla., Const., art. x, § 2; Ill., An. St., 1885, c. 3, ¶¶ 74–76; Ind., An. St., 1894, §§ 2419, 2424; Ky.. Stat., 1894, § 1403, ¶ 5; Mass., P. S., 1882, c. 135, §§ 1, 2; Mich., An. St., 1882, § 5847; Minn., G. S., 1894, § 4477; Miss., An. Code, 1892, § 1877; N. H., P. S., 1891, c. 195, §§ 1, 2; N. Y., Laws, 1896, c. 547, § 184; N. C., Code, 1883, §§ 2116, 2118; Ohio, R. S., 1891, §§ 6040, 6078, 6079; Oreg., An. St., 1887, §§ 1126–1129; Penn., Dig., 1883, p. 623, § 3; R. I., G. L., 1896, c. 214, § 4; Tenn., Code, 1884, §§3125–3128, 2934; Texas, R. S., 1895, arts. 2037–2039, 2046–2056; Vt., Stat., 1894, §§ 2418, 2419; Va., Code, 1887, § 3640; W. Va., Code, 1891, c. 41, § 27; Wis., An. St., 1889, § 3935.

[8] Ala., Code, 1896, §§ 2033, 2069; Ark., Dig. Stat., 1894, § 3694; Fla., Const., art. x, § 2; Me., R. S., 1883, c. 81, §§ 63–66; Mass., P. S., 1882, c. 123, §8 ; Mich., An. St., 1882, §§ 7728, 7729; Mo., R. S., 1899, §§ 3620, 3621; N. J., Rev., 1877, p. 1055, § 1; N. Y., C. C. P., § 1400; N. C., Const., art. x, §§ 3, 5; Ohio, R. S., 1881, § 5437, Stat., May 18, 1894, Acts, p. 307; Oreg., An. St., 1887, §§ 1126, 1127; S. C., C. S. L., 1893, § 2129; Tenn., Code, 1884, § 2943; Vt., Stat., 1894, §§ 2183–2185; Va., Code, 1887, §§ 3635, 3637; .Wis., An. St., 1889, § 2271.

[9] Ariz., R. S., 1887, § 1094; an additional allowance may be made for widow in case of need, *ibid.*, §§ 1095–1099; Cal., substantially same as Ariz. (C. C. P., §§ 1463–1470); Geo., Code, 1895, § 3465; Idaho, substantially same as Ariz. (R. S., 1887, §§ 5441–5446); Iowa, Code, 1897, §§ 3376, 3312, 3314; Kans., G. S., 1889, §§ 2833, 2619; Me., R. S., 1883, c. 65, §§ 21, 23, 26, c. 66, §1; Md., P. G. L., 1888, §§ 298, 299 gives allowance to widow; Laws, 1898, c. 331, § 3, extends provisions to surviving husband; Mo., R. S., 1889, §§ 105-109 gives allowance to widow to be deducted from her share in personal estate. An act of Apl. 8. 1895 (Laws, p. 35), extends provisions to widower, if the wife dies intestate, but the allowance is not deducted from his intestate share (see R. S., 1899, §§ 105-109, 111); Mont., substantially same as Ariz. (C. C. P., 1895, §§ 2581-2586); Neb. C. S., 1891, § 1235; Nev., substantially same as Ariz. (G. S., 1885, §§ 542, 2790-2796); N. J., Rev., 1877, p. 762, § 52; N. M., C. L. 1897, §§ 2041, 1993, 1994; Oklah.,

homestead [10] apply to the survivor, whether widow or widower.

substantially same as Ariz. (R. S., 1893, §§ 1300–1308); S. D., substantially
same as Ariz. (C. L., 1887, §§ 5779–5786); Utah, R. S., 1898, § 2831; Wy., substantially same as Ariz. (Laws, 1890–91, no. 70, c. xiii, §§ 1–7).

[10] Ariz., R. S., 1887, §§ 1094, 1100; Cal., C. C. P., §§ 1465, 1474, C. C., § 1265;
Col., An. St., 1891, § 2135; Conn., G. S., 1888, § 2783; Idaho, R. S., 1887, § 5441;
Ill., An. St., 1885, c. 52, ¶ 2; Iowa, Code, 1897, § 2985; Kans., G. S., 1889,
§§ 2595, 2619; Ky., Stat., 1894, §§ 1706, 1708; La., Const., art. 244; Minn., G. S,
1894, § 4470; Mont., C. C. P., 1895, §§ 2581, 2584, C. C., 1895, §§ 1703; Neb.,
C. S., 1891, § 1124; Nev., G. S., 1885, §§ 542, 2790; N. H., P. S., 1891, c. 138, §§ 2,
5; N. M., C. L., 1897, §§ 1749, 1994; N. D., R. C., 1895, § 3626; Oklah., R. S.,
1893, §§ 1300, 1302; S. D., C. L., 1887, §§ 5779–5781; Texas, R. S., 1895, arts.
2057–2062; Utah, R. S., 1898, § 2831; Wy., R. S., 1887, § 2782, Laws, 1890–91,
no. 70, c. xiii, § 8.

APPENDIX.

NOTE A. (See § 38, note 19.)

Miss., An. Code, 1892, § 2289. Married women are fully emancipated from all ·disability on account of coverture, and the common law, as to the disabilities of married women and its effect on the rights of property of the wife is totally abrogated, and marriage shall not impose any disability or incapacity on a woman as to ownership, acquisition, or disposition of property of any sort, or as to her capacity to make contracts and do all acts in reference to property which she could lawfully do if she were not married; but every woman now married or hereafter to be married, shall have the same capacity to acquire, hold, manage, control, use, enjoy and dispose of all property, real and personal, in possession or expectancy, and to make any contract in reference to it, and to bind herself personally, and to sue and be sued, with all the rights and liabilities incident thereto, as if she were not married.

NOTE B. (See § 38, note 21.)

Ohio, R. S., 1891, § 3144. A married person may take, hold and dispose of property, real or personal, the same as if unmarried.

Penn., Act of June 8, 1893 (Laws, p. 344), § 1. Hereafter a married woman shall have the same right and power as an unmarried person to acquire, o·vn, possess, control, use, lease, sell or otherwise dispose of any property of any kind, real, personal or mixed, and either in possession or expectancy, and may exercise the said right and power in the same manner, and to the same extent as an unmarried person, but she may not mortgage or convey her real property, unless her husband join in such mortgage or conveyance.

England. Act, § 45 & 46 Vict., C. 75, § 2. Every woman who marries after the commencement of this Act shall be entitled to have and hold as her separate property, and to dispose of in manner aforesaid all real and personal property which shall belong to her at the time of marriage, or shall be acquired by or devolve upon her after marriage, including any wages, earnings, money, and property gained or acquired by her in any employment, trade, or occupation in which she is engaged, or which she carries on separately from her husband, or by the exercise of any literary, artistic or scientific skill.

NOTE C. (See § 38, note 22.)

Mich., An. St.. 1882, § 6295. The real and personal estate of every female,

178
[178

acquired before marriage, and all property to which she may afterwards become entitled by gift, grant, inheritance, devise or in any other manner, shall be and remain the estate and property of such female, and shall not be liable for the debts, obligations or engagements of her husband, and may be contracted, sold, transferred, mortgaged, conveyed, devised or bequeathed by her as if she were unmarried.

NOTE D.   (See § 38, note 23.)

Dist. of Col., Act of June 1, 1896 (U. S. Stat. at Large, Vol. 29, p. 193), § 1.
The property, real and personal, which any woman in the District of Columbia may own at the time of her marriage, and the rents, issues, profits or proceeds thereof, and real, personal or mixed property which shall come to her by descent, devise, purchase or bequest, or the gift of any person, shall be and remain her sole and separate property notwithstanding her marriage, and shall not be subject to the disposal of her husband or liable for his debts, except that such property as shall come to her by gift of her husband shall be subject to, and liable for, the debts of the husband existing at the time of the gift.

NOTE E.   (See § 38, note 24.)

Col., An. St., 1891, § 3007. The property, real and personal, which any woman in this State may own at the time of her marriage, and the rents, issues, profits, and proceeds thereof, and any real, personal or mixed property which shall come to her by descent, devise or bequest, or the gift of any person except her husband, including presents or gifts from her husband, as jewelry, silver, tableware, watches, money and wearing apparel, shall remain her sole and separate property, notwithstanding her marriage, and not be subject to the disposal of her husband or liable for his debts.

NOTE F.   (See § 40, note 7.)

Soliloquy of an old lawyer occasioned by the abolition of dower and curtesy in Mississippi (quoted in Miss., An. Code, 1892, p. 573, note) : "Venerable relics of antiquity, you have come down to us from a former generation. You have survived the wreck of empires and change of dynasties. Born away back in the womb of time, whereof the memory of man runneth not to the contrary, you have outlived the war of the Roses, passed safely through the Protectorate, crossed the ocean, survived the great American Revolution, and rode out the storm of the late great war. Whatever attendants were absent from the bridal altar, you two, at least, were always there; and when the bride and groom mutually murmured, 'with all my worldly goods I thee endow,' you, as priest and priestess, sealed the covenant. Like shades, you've followed the twain blended into one, and when either fell, one of you administered the balm of consolation to the survivor. If pure religion and undefiled be to visit the fatherless and the widow in their affliction, thy mission has been akin to it. Venerable priest and priestess of the common law, farewell! You have been pleasant in your lives, and in death have not been divided."

LIST OF STATUTES WITH EXPLANATION OF SOME OF THE ABBREVIATIONS USED IN REFERENCES.

Acts, ... Vict.—The Public General Statutes passed in the ... year of the reign of Her Majesty Queen Victoria.

Ala., Code, 1896.—Alabama. Code of 1896.

An. étran.—Annuaire de Législation Étrangère. Paris.

An. fran.—Annuaire de Législation Française. Paris.

Ariz., R. S., 1887.—Arizona. Revised Statutes of 1887.

Ark., Dig. Stat., 1894.—Arkansas. Digest of the Statutes of 1894.

Austria, B. G.—Das allgemeine bürgerliche Gesetzbuch für das Kaiserthum Oesterreich. Vienna, 1883.

Austria, R. G. Bl.—Reichs-Gesetz-Blatt für das Kaiserthum Oesterreich.

—— Reichsgesetzblatt für die in Reichsrathe vertr. Königreiche und Länder.

Basle, Stat., Mch. 10, 1884.—Kanton Baselstadt. Gesetz betreffend eheliches Güterrecht, Erbrecht und Schenkungen. References are to translation in An. étran., Vol. 14, p. 545 *seq.*

Bull. des lois.—Bulletin des lois de la République Française. Paris.

Cal., C. C.—California. Code as amended to 1885.

Cal., C. C. P.—California. Code of Civil Procedure.

Cod.—Codex Justinianus recognovit Paulus Krueger. Berolini, 1895.

Col., An. St., 1891.—Colorado. Mill's Annotated Statutes of 1891.

Conn., G. S., 1888.—Connecticut. General Statutes of 1888.

Del., R. C., 1893.—Delaware. Revised Code of 1852 as amended to 1893.

Dig.—Digesta recognovit Theodorus Mommsen. Berolini, 1893.

Dist. of Col., R. S., 1873–74.—Revised Statutes of the United States relating to the District of Columbia......passed at the first session of the 43d Congress. Washington, 1875.

I. Entwurf.—Entwurf eines bürgerlichen Gesetzbuchs für das Deutsche Reich. Berlin, 1888.

II. Entwurf.—Entwurf eines Bürgerlichen Gesetzbuchs für das Deutsche Reich. Zweite Lesung. Nach dem Beschlusse der Redaktionskommission. Berlin, 1894.

III. Entwurf.—Entwurf eines Bürgerlichen Gesetzbuchs. Dem Reichstage vorgelegt in der vierten Session der neunten Legislaturperiode. Berlin, 1896.

Finland, Stat., Apl. 15, 1889—Finland. Lag om makars egendoms och gölds. References are to translation in An. étran., vol. 19, p. 821 *seq.*

Fla., R. S., 1892.—Florida. Revised Statutes of 1892.

France, C. C., C. C. P., Code de Com.—France. Code civil, code de procédure civile, code de commerce. References are to Codes Français et Lois Usuelles, par. H. F. Riviére. Paris, 1881.

Geo., Code, 1895.—Georgia. Code of 1895.

Germany, B. G.—Das Bürgerliche Gesetzbuch nebst dem Einführungsgesetze für
    das Deutsche Reich. Leipzig, 1896.

Germany, R. G. Bl.—Reichsgesetzblatt. Berlin.

Glaris, L. B.—Landsbuch des Kantons Glarus. References are to translation in
    An. étran., Vol. 14, p. 510 *seq.*

Hawaii, C. L., 1884.—Hawaii. Compiled Laws of 1884.

Idaho, R. S., 1887.—Idaho. Revised Statutes of 1887.

Ill., An. St., 1885.—Illinois. Starr and Curtis' Annotated Statutes of 1885.

Ind., An. St., 1894.—Indiana. Burns' Annotated Statutes. Revision of 1894.

Inst.—Institutiones recognovit Paulus Krueger. Berolini, 1893.

Iowa, Code, 1897.—Iowa. Code of 1897.

Italy, C. C.—Le Code Civil Italien. Traduction complète du Code Civil Italien
    par M. Joseph Orsier. Paris, 1868.

Kans., G. S., 1889.—Kansas. General Statutes of 1889.

Ky., Stat., 1894.—Kentucky. Barbour and Carroll's Statutes of 1894.

La., C. C.—Louisiana. Saunder's Civil Code revised to 1889.

Lucerne, Stat., Nov. 26, 1880.—Kanton Luzern. Gesetz über die ehelichen Vor-
    mundschaft. References are to translation in An. étran., Vol. 10, p.
    486 *seq.*

Me., R. S., 1883.—Maine. Revised Statutes of 1883.

Md., P. G. L., 1888.—Maryland. Public General Laws of 1888.

Mass., P. S., 1882.—Massachusetts. Public Statutes of 1882.

Mich., An. St., 1882.—Michigan. Howell's Annotated Statutes of 1882.

Minn., G. S., 1894.—Minnesota. Wenzell's General Statutes of 1894.

Miss., An. Code, 1892.—Mississippi. Annotated Code of 1892.

Mo., R. S., 1899.—Missouri. Revised Statutes of 1899.

Mont., C. C., C. C. P., 1895.—Montana. Civil Code, Code of Civil Procedure.
    Saunder's Codes and Statutes of 1895.

Neb., C. S., 1891.—Nebraska. Cobbey's Consolidated Statutes of 1891.

Nev., G. S., 1885.—Nevada. General Statutes of 1885.

N. H., P. S., 1891.—New Hampshire. Public Statutes of 1891.

N. J., Rev., 1877.—New Jersey. Revision of 1877.

N. M., C. L., 1897.—New Mexico. Compiled Laws of 1897.

N. Y., C. C. P.—New York. Throop's Code of Civil Procedure of 1885.

N. Y., R. S., 1889.—New York. Revised Statutes of 1889.

N. C., Code, 1883.—North Carolina. Code of 1883.

N. D., R. C., 1895.—North Dakota. Revised Code of 1895.

Norway, Stat., June 29, 1888.—Norway. Lov om Formuesforholdet mellen Aegte-
    feller. References are to translation in An. étran., Vol. 18, p. 762 *seq.*

Nov.—Novellae recognovit Rudolphus Schoell et Guilelmus Kroll. Berolini, 1895.

Ohio, R. S., 1891.—Ohio. Smith and Benedict's Revised Statutes of 1891.

Oklah., R. S., 1893. – Oklahoma. Revised Statutes of 1893.

Oreg., An. Laws, 1887.—Oregon. Hill's Annotated Laws of 1887.

Penn., Dig., 1883.—Pennsylvania. Brightly's Purdon's Digest, 1700–1883.

Prussia, A. L. R.—Allgemeines Landrecht für die Preussischen Staaten nebst den ergänzenden und abändernden Bestimmungen der Reichs und Landesgesetzgebung. Mit Erläuterungen von H. Rehbein und O. Remcke. Berlin, 1880.

Prussia, G. S. S.—Gesetz–Sammlung für die Königlich Preussischen Staaten.

R. I., G. L., 1896.—Rhode Island. General Laws of 1896.

Saxony, B. G.—Das Bürgerliche ·Gesetzbuch für das Königreich Sachsen nebst den damit in Verbindung stehenden Reichs- und Landesgesetzen. Von Dr. Eduard Siebenhaar. Fünfte Auflage. Leipzig, 1883.

Sirey, Recuéil.—Recuéil Général des Lois et des Arrêts en matière civil, criminnelle, administrative et de droit public. Fonde par J. B. Sirey. Paris.

S. C., C. S. L., 1893.—South Carolina. Civil Statute Laws of 1893.

S. D., C. L., 1887. South Dakota. Dakota Compiled Laws of 1887.

Spain, C. C.—Code Civil Espagnol. Traduit et annoté par A. Levé. Paris, 1890.

Sweden, F.-S.—Swensk Författnings-Sammling. Stockholm.

Switz., Stat., June 14, 1881.—Switzerland. Bundesgesetz über das Obligationenrecht vom 14 Brachmonat, 1881. Bern, 1881.

Switz., Vorentwurf,—Vorentwurf Bundesgesetz über das Privatrecht. Schweizerisches Civilgesetzbuch. Erster und zweiter Teil. Personen- und Familienrecht.

Tenn., Code, 1884.—Tennessee. Milliken and Vertres' Code of 1884.

Texas, R. S., 1895.—Texas. Revised Statutes of 1895.

U. S. Stat. at Large.—The Statutes at Large of the United States of America. Washington.

Utah, R. S., 1898.—Utah. Revised Statutes of 1898.

Vt., Stat., 1894.—Vermont. Statutes of 1894.

Va., Code, 1887.—Virginia. Code of 1887.

Wash., G. S., 1891.—Washington. Hill's General Statutes of 1891.

Wash., C. P., 1891.—Washington. Code of Procedure of 1891.

W. Va., Code, 1891.—West Virginia. Code of 1891.

Wis., An. St., 1889.—Wisconsin. Sanborn and Berryman's Annotated Statutes of 1889.

Wy., R. S., 1887.—Wyoming. Revised Statutes of 1887.

Zürich, P. R. G.—Privatrechtliches Gesetzbuch für den Kanton Zürich. Auf Grundlage des Bluntschli'schen Kommentars allgemeinfasslich erläutert, durch Dr. A. Schneider, Redaktor des Gesetzes. Zürich, 1888.

LIST OF AUTHORITIES.

Alexander, J., *Konkursgesetze aller Länder der Erde*. Berlin, 1892 (Cited as Alexander, *Konk-G.*)

Archiv für bürgerliches Recht, herausgegeben von J. Kohler und B. Ring. Berlin. (Cited as *Arch. f. bürg. Recht.*)

Archiv für die civilistische Praxis, herausgegeben von Degenkolb, Franklin, *etc.* Freiburg i/B. (Cited as *Arch. f. d. civ. Prax.*)

Bechmann, Dr. August, *Das Römische Dotalrecht.* Erlangen, 1863, 1867. (Cited as Bechmann, *Dotalrecht.*)

Beiträge zur Erläuterung des Deutschen Rechts, in besonderer Beziehung auf das Preussische Recht, herasusgegeben von Rassow und Küntzel. Berlin. (Cited as *Beitr. z. Erl. des deut. Rechts.*)

Blackstone, Sir William, *Commentaries on the Laws of England.* With notes by Thomas M. Cooley. Third Edition. Chicago, 1884. (Cited as Blackstone, *Comm.*)

Bridel, Louis, *Le Droit de la Femme mariée sur le Produit de son Travail.* Genève, 1893. (Cited as Bridel, *Femme mariée.*)

Buckstaff, Florence G., " Married Women's Property in Anglo-Saxon and Anglo-Norman Law and the Origin of the Common Law Dower." In *Annals of the American Academy of Political and Social Science,* vol. iv, p. 247.

Bulletin de la Société de Législation Comparée. Paris. (Cited as *Bull. lég. comp.*)

Das deutsche Recht und die deutschen Frauen. Kritische Beleuchtung des Entwurfes eines bürgerlichen Gesetzbuchs für das deutsche Reich. Herausgegeben vom Rechtsschutzverein für Frauen in Dresden. Frankenburg, Sachsen, 1895.

Denkschrift zum Entwurf eines bürgerlichen Gesetzbuchs nebst drei Anlagen. Dem Reichstage vorgelegt in der vierten Session der neunten Legislaturperiode. Berlin, 1896. (Cited as *Denkschrift.*)

Dernburg, Heinrich. *Pandekten.* Fünfte Auflage. Berlin, 1897.

Dunscomb, S. Whitney, *Bankruptcy.* In Columbia College Studies in History, Economics and Public Law, Vol. II. New York, 1893.

Essays in Anglo-Saxon Law. Boston, 1876.

Gide, Paul, *Etude sur la Condition privée de la Femme dans le Droit Ancien et moderne et en particulier sur la Senatus Consulte Velléien.* Paris, 1867.

Gierke, Otto, *Der Entwurf eines bürgerlichen Gesetzbuchs und das deutsche Recht.* Leipzig, 1889. (Cited as Gierke, *Entwurf.*)

Guntzberger, A., *De l'Extension des Droits de la Femme Mariée sur les Produits de son Industrie Personelle.* Paris, 1896. (Cited as Guntzberger.)

Heusler, Andreas, *Institutionen des Deutschen Privatrechts.* Leipzig, 1895. (Cited as Heusler, *Inst.*)

Huc, M. Théophile, *Le Code Civil Italien et le Code Napoléon.* Deuxième édition· Paris, 1868. (Cited as Huc, *Code Civil Italien.*)

Kent, James, *Commentaries on American Law.* 13th Edition, Boston, 1884. (Cited as Kent, *Comm.*)

Lehr, Ernest, *Éléments de Droit Civil Russe.* Paris, 1877. (Cited as Lehr, *Droit Russe.*)

Leuthold, Dr. C. E. *Russische Rechtskunde.* Systematische Darstellung des in Russland geltenden Privat- Handels- und Strafrechts, sowie des Prozesses. Leipzig, 1889. (Cited as Leuthold, *R. R.*)

Lardy, C., *Les Législations civiles des Cantons Suisses en Matière de Tutelle, de Régime Matrimonial quant aux Biens et de Succession.* Deuxième édition. Paris, 1877. (Cited as Lardy, *Législations Suisses.*)

Motive zu dem Entwurfe eines Bürgerlichen Gesetzbuchs für das Deutsche Reich. Berlin und Leipzig, 1888. (Cited as *Motive.*)

Muirhead, James, *Historical Introduction to the Private Law of Rome.* Edinburgh, 1886. (Cited as Muirhead, *Roman Law.*)

Neubauer, *Das eheliche Güterrecht des Auslandes nebst Mittheilungen über das in den Vereinigten Staaten von Nord-Amerika geltende Erbrecht.* Berlin, 1882. (Cited as Neubauer, *Ausland.*)

Neubauer, *Das in Deutschland geltende eheliche Güterrecht.* Nach amtlichen Materialien. Zweite Auflage, Berlin, 1889. (Cited as Neubauer, *Deutschland.*)

Pascaud, H., " Le droit de la Femme mariée aux Produits de son Travail." In *Revue Politique et Parlementaire,* vol. ix, p. 568.

Pollock, Sir Frederick and Maitland, Frederick William, *The History of English Law before the time of Edward I.* Cambridge, 1895. (Cited as Pol. and Mait., *Hist.*)

Proelz, Sera und Raschke, Marie, *Die Frau im neuen bürgerlichen Gesetzbuch.* Berlin, 1895.

Schouler, James, *A Treatise on the Law of Husband and Wife.* Boston, 1882. (Cited as Schouler, *H. & W.*)

Schröder, Dr. Richard, *Lehrbuch der Deutschen Rechtsgeschichte.* Dritte Auflage. Leipzig, 1898. (Cited as Schröder, *Lehrbuch.*)

Sohm, Rudolph, *Institutionen. Ein Lehrbuch der Geschichte und des System des Römischen Privatrechts.* Siebente Auflage. Leipzig, 1898. (Cited as Sohm, *Inst.*)

Viollet, Paul, *Précis de l'Histoire du Droit Français.* Paris, 1886. (Cited as Viollet, *Précis.*)

Windscheid, Dr. Bernhard, *Lehrbuch des Pandektenrechts.* Siebente Auflage. Frankfurt a/M., 1891. (Cited as Windscheid, *Pandekten.*)

Zeitschrift für das Privat- und öffentliche Recht der Gegenwart, herausgegeben von Dr. C. S. Grünhut. Wien. (Cited as *Zeit. f. d. Privat- u. öff. Recht*).

INDEX.

[References are to pages, but the notes must be examined where the index refers to the legislation of particular states.]

wife's incapacity to conduct legal proceedings under, 44; wife's contracts for necessities under, 46, 47; property relations of husband and wife under, 97–9, 125; abrogation of, as regards wife's property, 131, 132; succession of married parties under, 157, 162.

English Equity Rules, wife's contractual power under, 28, 29; wife's separate property under, 28, 29, 125–8; restraint upon anticipation under, 29; gifts between married parties under, 41; wife's equity to a settlement under, 125, 126.

Exclusive Rights of Husband, System of. See Individual Property Systems.

Exempt Personal Property, wife's right to hold, 141; wife's consent essential to mortgage of, 141; succession to, 175, 176.

Fiction of Unity, in English Common Law, 27, 40.

Finland, gifts between married parties in, 40; wife's capacity to sue and be sued in, 44; wife's right and duty of household administration in, 46; marriage agreements in, 53–5, 60; post-nuptial agreements restricted in, 54, 55; statutory system in, 57, 59; establishment of system of separate property by contract prohibited in, 60; system of community in, 59, 67, 68, 71, 72, 77, 78, 81–3, 87–9, 92, 93; dotal property in, 68, 85, 87; earnings of wife in, 71, 72, 135; separate property in, 85, 87, 124, 146; common property in, 67, 68, 72, 77, 81, 82, 93; obligations of married parties in, 77, 78; system of separate property in, 60, 124, 146, 149; support of family in, 149.

France, wife's general contractual capacity in, 19–21; marriage agreements in, 20, 53–5, 57, 60–2, 66, 67, 100; post-nuptial marriage agreements restricted in, 20, 54, 55; wife's right to make deposits in banks in, 21, 73; wife's right to become member of mutual benefit society in, 21; gifts between married parties in, 38, 40; wife as a trader in, 41, 42; wife's capacity to sue and be sued in, 43, 44; types of limited community in, 51; statutory and contractual systems in, 55, 57, 58; general community in, 58, 65–7, 71–7, 81–94; community of movables and acquisitions in, 58, 67, 68, 71–4, 77, 81–94; community of acquisitions in, 58, 68–74, 78–94; system of separate property in, 58, 93, 113, 124, 135, 142, 143, 146–150; system of marital administration and usufruct in, 58, 99, 100, 103, 106–9, 111, 113; system of dowry in, 58, 114–6, 118–24; separate property in, 21, 64, 67, 69, 85, 87, 100, 116, 124, 142, 143, 146, 147; dotal property in, 64, 66–8, 85, 87, 99, 100, 103, 106-9, 114–6, 118–24; common property in, 65, 66, 68–71, 73–87, 91–4; earnings of wife in, 71, 73, 74, 115, 135, 136; obligations of married parties in, 75–80, 107, 108, 153; support of family in, 147–50; alimony in, 152: intestate succession in, 158, 159; legal portion in, 169, 170; provision for support of survivor in, 174, 175.

General Community of Property, system of. See Community Property Systems.

Geneva, statutory and contractual systems in, 58; earnings of wife in, 71, 73; see also Swiss Cantons.

German Draft Codes, wife's contracts for personal service in, 25, 26; names given

System of Separate Property, defined, 52; obtains as statutory or contractual system, 58, 59, 124; frauds upon creditors promoted by, 37; development of, by Court of Chancery, 125, 126; by legislation in England and United States, 128–30; necessity for statutory definition of, 127; constitutional provisions establishing, 128, 129; different methods of statutory definition of, 131–4, 178, 179; general character of wife's property under, 131, 132, 134, 135; gifts from husband to wife under, 37, 132, 133; wife's interest in insurance policies upon husband's life under, 37, 38, 133, 134; wife's earnings under, 135–7; husband's administration of wife's property under, 134, 143; wife's right of administration under, 142–7; support of family under, 147–53; effects of divorce under, 150–2; liability for obligations under, 153, 154; attitude of, towards legal portion, 171–3; see also, Dower and Curtesy, Exempt Personal Property, Homestead. See also, Succession of Married Parties, Provision for Support of Survivor.

Inheritance. See Succession of Married Parties.

Insurance Policies, wife's power to effect and dispose of, 33, 34; limit of, upon husband's life for benefit of wife, 37, 38, 133; separate property in, 66, 128, 133; effect of fraud upon, 134.

Inventory, of wife's property, 87, 109.

Italy, wife's general legal capacity in draft code of, 21; wife's contractual capacity in, 21, 22; contracts between married parties in, 22; gifts between married parties in, 40; wife's capacity to sue and be sued in, 44; marriage agreements in, 22, 53–5, 57, 60–2; post-nuptial marriage agreements restricted in, 22, 54, 55; statutory and contractual systems in, 55, 57, 58, 60; establishment of community other than of acquisitions prohibited in, 60; community of acquisitions in, 58, 68–71, 78–83, 85–92; common property in, 68–71, 78–83, 91, 92; dotal property in, 68–70, 85, 87, 114–6, 118–24; separate property in, 70, 85, 87, 116, 135, 142–4, 146; earnings of wife in, 71, 116, 135; obligations of married parties in, 78–80; system of dowry in, 58, 114–6, 118–24; system of separate property in, 135, 142–4, 146, 148–50; support of the family in, 148–50; alimony in, 152; intestate succession in, 160; legal portion in, 169, 170; provision for support of widow in, 174–5.

Judicial Authorization, essential to contracts of wife, 19, 20, 22–6, 33, 36; may supply husband's consent, 19, 20, 22, 24, 26, 47, 84, 107; essential for wife to become a trader, 42; essential for marriage agreements, 61; may supply wife's consent, 83, 106.

Legal Capacity of Married Woman, influenced by matrimonial property relations, 16, 21, 23, 24; general, 16–9; explanation of limitations upon, 18–23; general contractual, 19–34; to contract with husband, 20, 22–8, 31–4; to be a trader, 41–3; to become surety, 34–6; to sue and be sued, 43–5; to administer household affairs, 46–8.

Legal Mortgage, for protection of wife's property, 120, 121.

Legal Portion, marriage agreements cannot modify, 62; nature of, 168, 169; attitude of Roman law respecting, 169; where community is statutory system, 169, 170, 173; where dowry is statutory system, 170; where marital administration and usufruct is statutory system, 170, 171; where separate property is statutory system, 171–3; tendency to make, same as intestate share, 171, 172.

Limitation of Actions, exemption of wife from operation of, 45–46.

Louisiana, wife's contractual capacity in, 22; wife's power to become surety in, 35; wife as a trader in, 43; wife's capacity to sue and be sued in, 44; marriage agreements in, 53–5, 60–2; post-nuptial marriage agreements restricted in, 54; statutory and contractual systems in, 57, 59; community of acquisitions in, 59, 68, 69, 79–89, 91, 93; common property in, 68, 69, 79–87, 91, 93; dotal property in, 68, 69, 85, 87, 114–6, 118–24; separate property in, 68, 85, 87, 116, 124, 135, 142–44, 146, 147; earnings of wife in, 116; obligations of married parties in, 79, 80: system of dowry in, 59, 114–6, 118–24; system of separate property in, 124, 135, 142–4, 146–9; support of the family in, 148, 149; intestate succession in, 159, 160; legal portion in, 169, 170; provision for support of survivor in, 174, 175.

Lucerne, wife's right of household administration in, 47; statutory system in, 58; see also, Swiss Cantons.

Marital Administration and Usufruct, system of, see Individual Property Systems.

Marital Authorization, essential to wife's contracts, 19–26, 32, 33; supplied by the court, 19, 22, 24–6, 44, 84, 107; not required for revocation of gifts, 40; for acceptance or rejection of gifts, successions, etc., 106, 107; essential for wife to become a trader, 41; for alienation of property, 144–7; for civil proceedings by wife, 43, 44; for wife's acts affecting common property, 84; for wife's acts affecting dotal property, 106; for wife's acts affecting separate property, 142, 145–7; for disposition of homestead, 142.

Marriage Agreements, freedom to contract, 53–5; ante-nuptial, 53, 54; post-nuptial, 54, 55; special form for, 60, 61; publication of, 61; register for, 61; affecting order of succession, 61, 62; affecting legal portion, 62; dissolution of community by, 89; establishment of dotal property by, 66; establishment of separate property by, 66–68, 100; termination of marital administration and usufruct by, 111; for return of dowry, 122.

Married Woman. See Wife.

Married Women's Property Acts. See Separate Property, Wife.

Matrimonial Property Register, 61.

Matrimonial Property Systems, affected by conceptions of personal status of married parties, 16; changes made during nineteenth century in, 11–4; tendency towards development of common regulations in, 14; classification of, 49–52; table showing territorial distribution of, 57–9; determination of, by marriage agreement, 53–5, 57–60; determination of, by statute, 55–9; number of, in Germany before adoption of national code, 56; proposals to define different, in code of Germany, 56; see also, Community Property Systems, Individual Property Systems.

Minority of Husband. See Incapacity of Husband.

Mortgage, legal, of husband's immovables for protection of wife's property, 109, 120, 121.

Movables, community of, and acquisitions. See Community Property Systems.

Mutual Benefit Associations, married woman as a member of, 21, 33, 34.

Necessaries, wife's contracts for, 46, 47.

Norway, wife's general legal capacity in, 18; wife's contractual capacity in, 27; wife's power to become surety in, 36; gifts between married parties in, 40; marriage agreements in, 53, 55, 57, 60, 61, 66, 67, 89; statutory and contractual systems in, 55, 57, 59; common property in, 66, 75, 76, 81–7, 91, 92; separate property in, 66, 67, 85, 87, 124, 135, 142, 144; dotal property in, 66, 85, 87; general community in, 59, 66, 67, 71, 75–7, 81–9, 91, 92; earnings of wife in, 71, 135; obligations of married parties in, 75–7; system of separate property in, 59, 124, 135, 142–4.

Obligations of Married Parties, liability of community for, 75–80, 91; individual liability for, 76–8, 80, 91–3, 95–7, 107, 108; arising from illegal acts, 76, 80, 108, 153, 154; arising from administration of separate property, 76; liability for ante-nuptial, 79, 153; liability for post-nuptial, 79, 80, 153, 154 liability of dotal property for, 108; liability for, under system of separate property, 153, 154.

Paraphernalia. See Dowry and Separate Property under Individual Property Systems.

Personal Property, wife's consent essential to mortgage of exempt, 141; succession to exempt, 175–7; particular rules of succession to, 161, 162, 167.

Personal Service, wife's contracts for, 24–6, 32–4.

Presumption as to Ownership of Movables, 38, 39; of objects intended for personal use of wife, 39; of property under community systems, 38, 70; rebutted by inventory, 87, 109.

Products of Personal Industry of Wife. See Earnings of Wife.

Protection of Wife's Property, under community systems, 86, 87; under marital administration and usufruct, 109, 110; under system of dowry, 115, 117, 120, 121; right to demand security for, 109, 121; right to register mortgage over husband's immovables for, 109, 121; privileges in husband's bankruptcy for, 109, 110; legal mortgage for, 120, 121.

Provision for Support of Survivor, importance of, 173, 174; where community is the statutory system, 174; where dowry is the statutory system, 174, 175; in United States, 175–7; restricted to widow, 175, 176.

Prussia, wife's contractual capacity in, 24, 25; marriage agreements in, 25, 53, 55, 57, 60–2, 66, 67, 89, 111; code of, supplanted by national code, 24; wife's power to become surety in, 36; gifts between married parties in, 40; wife as a trader in, 41; wife's capacity to sue and be sued in, 44; wife's right of household administration in, 47; statutory and contractual systems in, 55–7, 59; separate property in 24, 64, 67–9, 85, 87, 100, 101, 107–9, 124, 135, 142–4; dotal property in, 64–9, 85, 87, 99, 103, 106–9, 111–3; common property in, 65, 66, 68–70, 72, 75, 76, 78–87, 91–4; general community in, 59, 65–7, 72, 75–7, 81–94; community of acquisitions in, 59, 68–70, 72, 78, 94; marital administration and usufruct in, 59, 99–103, 106–9, 111–3; system of separate property in, 59, 124, 135, 142–4; earnings of wife in, 71, 72, 101, 135; obligations of married parties in, 75–80, 107; intestate succession in, 160, 161; legal portion in, 169, 171.

Real Property. See Immovables.

Restraint upon Anticipation, 29, 30.

Roman Law, wife's general legal capacity in, 16, 17; wife's contractual capacity in, 26, 27; contracts between married parties in, 27; wife's power to become surety in, 34, 35; gifts between married parties in, 38, 40; property relations between married parties in, 12, 13, 95, 96, 114–8, 120, 122, 123; resistance to reception of, in family relations, 49, 55, 56; succession of married parties in, 155–7; legal portion in, 169; provision for support of widow in, 156, 169.

Russia, wife's general legal capacity in, 18; wife's contractual capacity in, 27; wife's power to draw bills of exchange in, 36; gifts between married parties in, 36, 40; wife as a trader in, 43; marriage agreements in, 53, 55, 60, 62; statutory system in, 56, 57, 59; system of separate property in, 59, 124, 135, 142–4; separate property in, 124, 127, 135, 142–4; earnings of wife in, 135; support of the family in, 150; intestate succession in, 161; legal portion in, 169–71.

Savings of Wife, deposit of, in banks, 21, 22, 28, 33, 34, 121, 134, 135; excluded from community, 65; see also, Earnings of Wife.

Saxony, wife's contractual capacity in, 24, 25; code of, supplanted by national code, 24; wife's power to become surety in, 36; gifts between married parties in, 40; wife as a trader in, 41; wife's capacity to sue and be sued in, 44; wife's right of household administration in, 47; marriage agreements in, 53, 55, 57, 60–2, 66, 67, 111; statutory and contractual systems in, 55, 57, 59; separate property in, 24, 64, 67, 85, 100, 101, 107–9, 124, 135, 142–4; dotal property in, 66, 85, 99–103, 106–9, 111–3; common property in, 65, 66, 72, 75, 78, 81–5, 87, 91, 93; community systems in, 59, 65–7, 72, 75, 78, 81–5, 87, 89–91, 93; marital administration and usufruct in, 59, 99–103, 106–9, 111–3; system of separate property in, 59, 124, 135, 142–4, 150; earnings of wife in, 71, 72, 101, 135; obligations of married parties in, 75, 78, 107, 109; support of husband by wife in, 150; intestate succession in, 160, 161; legal portion in, 169–71.

Scandinavian Countries, earnings of wife in, 71, 72; see also, Denmark, Norway, Sweden, Finland.

Separate Property, system of, see Individual Property Systems; terms used to designate, in community systems, 63, 64; defined, 63, 64; under general community, 65–7; under community of movables and acquisitions, 67, 69; under community of acquisitions, 68–70; under marital administration and usufruct, 99–101; under system of dowry, 116; development of, by Court of Chancery

125, 126; development of, by legislation, 128–30; in objects of personal use, 65, 100, 101; in wife' savings, 65, 128, 134, 135; in wife's earnings, 66, 74, 101, 116, 134–7; n policies of insurance, 37, 38, 66, 128, 133, 134; in gifts, 37, 66, 69, 100, 132–5; in successions, 66, 69, 100, 134; established by agreement, 66–8, 100; of husband not recognized under limited community, 69, 70; administration of, 85, 107, 127, 134, 142–7.

Separation of Property, under community systems, 87–94; under marital administration and usufruct, 110–3; under system of dowry, 121–4.

Spain, wife's contractual capacity in, 21, 22; marriage agreements in, 22, 53–5, 57, 60–62; gifts between married parties in, 40; wife's capacity to sue and be sued in, 44; wife's right of household management in, 46; post-nuptial marriage agreements restricted in, 54, 55; statutory and contractual systems in, 55, 57, 58; common property in, 68, 71, 78–87, 91–3; dotal property in, 69, 85, 87, 115, 116, 118–24; separate property in, 85, 87, 116, 124, 135, 142–4, 146, 147; community of acquisitions in, 58, 68, 69, 71, 78–89, 91–3; system of dowry in, 115, 116, 118–24; system of separate property in, 124, 135, 142–4, 146–50; earnings of wife in, 71, 135; obligations of married parties in, 78–80; support of the family in, 147–50; alimony in, 152; intestate succession in, 159; legal portion in, 169, 170; provision for support of widow in, 174, 175.

Statutory Property Systems, 55–60.

Succession of Married Parties, marriage agreements affecting, 61, 62; relation of law of, to matrimonial property rights, 15, 155–7; Roman law of, 155–7, 169: Teutonic law of, 156, 157; English common law of, 157, 162, 163; modern principles of, 157, 158; in French Civil Code, 158; recent statutory changes in, 158–60; where community is statutory system. 158–60, 169, 170, 174; where dowry is statutory system, 160, 170, 174, 175; where marital administration and usufruct is statutory system, 160, 161, 170, 171; where separate property is statutory system, 161–7, 171–3, 175–7; distinction between real and personal property in, 161, 162, 166, 167; distinction between husband and wife in, 162, 163, 166, 167, 171, 173, 175, 176; affected by number and degree of heirs, 159, 161, 162, 164–6; tendency to equalize shares of husband and wife in, 162, 163, 166, 167, 171, 176, 177; tendency to make legal portion same as intestate share in, 171, 172; see also, Legal Portion, Provision for Support of Survivor.

Sue and be Sued, wife's capacity to, 43–6.

Support of the Family, failure of husband to provide for, justifies separation of property, 88, 111, 122; by the husband, 108, 147; joint liability of husband and wife for, 148, 151; wife's duty to contribute to, 148, 149.

Surety, wife's power to become, 34–6.

Sweden, statutory system in, 59; earnings of wife in, 72.

Swiss Cantons, wife's contractual capacity in, 23; guardianship of women in, 23; marriage agreements in, 23, 53, 54, 60–2; wife's power to become surety in, 34; wife as a trader in, 41, 43; wife's right of household management